362.1968
THA

HOPE AND RECOVERY

A MOTHER-DAUGHTER
STORY ABOUT
ANOREXIA NERVOSA,
BULIMIA, AND
MANIC DEPRESSION

Hope and Recovery

& By Emma Lou Thayne
Becky Thayne Markosian

FRANKLIN WATTS
New York / London / Toronto / Sydney

ACKNOWLEDGMENTS

We would like to thank Dr. Bernard Grosser for his professional and caring guidance, Lavina Fielding Anderson for her interest and editing, Gerald A. Peterson for his letter of appreciation, our families for never failing to be there for us, and Paul Markosian for his love and faith.

Photographs copyright © Emma Lou Thayne

Permission to use "My dreams, my works, must wait 'til after hell" by Gwendolyn Brooks granted by Ms. Brooks.

For those who have such stories to tell,
in the hope for them of a happy ending

CONTENTS

HOPE AND RECOVERY

INTRODUCTION

In the 1980s and 1990s, the eating disorders anorexia and bulimia have become much-publicized health concerns among increasing numbers of Americans. Who has not known someone who starves and/or throws up and purges to maintain the unrealistic weight flaunted in the media as desirable? Young girls and women try to look like the fourteen-year-old bodies with mature heads pasted together in ads; young boys and men binge and purge to maintain an ideal weight for sports. An estimated 24 percent of our population indulges in fearsome dieting practices to feel accepted among their peers or by themselves. And with such consequences!

This is as true in our hometown of Salt Lake City, Utah, as it is all over the country. A few months before we started this book, Becky, my daughter, and I listened to a mother talk of the death of her bright, beautiful, far-from-fat sixteen-year-old daughter, who had taken baking soda to make throwing up easier. How much soda, doctors could only guess. But it swelled in her intestine and killed her. Listening, Becky broke down, and I convulsed with remembering.

At that same age, sixteen, Becky was doing equally dangerous and compulsive things to avoid her most intolerable torment—weighing more than 105 pounds. With her body build, doctors said a more reasonable weight would be about 115 pounds. But reason had nothing to do with Becky's outrageous dieting and the very real threat of death. Listening to that other mother, I put my arm gratefully around Becky, together in the agony we felt. I knew that we were way beyond lucky to have her alive, productive, and happy, now eighteen years from the terror she had left behind in the three years of her excruciating recovery. Her sickness was a triple threat of chemical imbalance, manic depression, and bulimia/anorexia. In what order they took over her system and how they influenced each other, no one is yet able to understand. Each was conquered in its own time, but the bulimia took the longest. It was what almost killed Becky.

In the 1970s, between the ages of thirteen and twenty-one, Becky was succumbing to and then reeling back from a disease that few knew anything about. After her return to a satisfying life, she was ashamed to discuss that period of irrationality. She asked me only a few months ago, "Weren't you embarrassed, Mom?"

My answer then was the same as now: "No. I was not embarrassed. Desperate, aching, consumed, overwhelmed, terrified—oh, I was so afraid—sometimes angry, inept, and sad, sad, sad, but not embarrassed." I felt she had a disease, like diabetes, or a damaged system, like appendicitis, that needed a medical cure before she could find her life and herself.

Never had I been in a bleaker time. Never had I felt less able, more panicky than when Becky's disease, so out of control, consumed every moment of my mothering, mothering that until then had seemed mostly easy and satisfying.

As parents, my husband, Mel, and I knew the guilt and torment of feeling somehow responsible for something we had pathetically little knowledge of or ability to make better. All we could do was what we could, and sometimes that seemed painfully feeble in dealing with what inundated and threatened the peace in all of our lives.

Even without understanding Becky's problem completely, most people understood enough so that they were wonderfully supportive. Her friends tried to be friends; her extended family wanted to help. Most of us blundered along, accepting even in our desperation. From others, Becky had to endure rumors and sometimes a medieval sense of mental or emotional illness. Such illness is never pleasant; sometimes it can cause cruel misunderstandings. A well-meaning church official, kind and sincere, offered to give Becky a blessing to get rid of her "evil spirits."

Fourteen years later, working in the young women's program of our Mormon Church, Becky learned of a number of girls who were captive to much of what she had survived. One day while giving a stained-glass demonstration to the whole group, she spontaneously told of having had manic depression and bulimia and of getting better. That was the first time she had ever admitted having the disease, and she felt relieved as she noted the interest and understanding the young women showed.

Last summer Becky called me and said, "Mom, I can help. I've worked with some of these girls, and they've listened to me—we've become friends. You remember I talked to two different girls about getting some help? Going to the hospital? Well, they're each doing better, but they're still battling the terrible addiction. And their mothers have called—they're the ones who suffer. In fact, the whole family suffers. What if we wrote my story, the two of us? Do you think it might do some good? What if we could give them some hope?"

Any power in the universe knows—Becky had to know—that her coming back from that so hopeless pit has colored my life—all of our lives—with a happiness that has pervaded the years since. What if only one girl or boy or one mother or father could find some relief in knowing that he or she was not alone, that it had happened to Becky and me?

Becky, now forty, has been married for eighteen years to a man she loves. She has three young sons and companionable friends. She creates stained glass as a vocation, has a job in real estate, plays the piano in a church organization, and lives in a home she manages with the same transitory joys, frustrations, and challenges of any wife and mother. Over the years, she has become a person with a sturdy sense of herself—she knows she is someone who deserves a good life and good health in a well body.

Becky is no longer imperiled by the dieting that nearly killed her and sent the rest of us into abject hopelessness. "Mom, in all these years, in the good times and the hard ones, I've never been tempted to go back to that horrible habit. That's what I never get over being grateful for, you know."

I do know. I feel the raging gratitude too—and anger, as the disease of wanting to be thin claims more and more unwary victims. I can blame advertisers and movies, peer pressure and TV. I can blame ignorance and a universal hunger for popularity. I can deplore the effects of parental expectation and sibling rivalries. I can despair at a Pepsi® Generation of instant gratification, to whom the shape of a body is the shape of self- or group approval. But what I know is that something else has to be seen as important in causing and curing the suffering.

And so this book is about Becky's turn-around from that dead-end sickness. She got better. So did I. It didn't happen without many mistakes. There wasn't much I could do except be there for her. Becky says, "I couldn't have made it without my mother. She never gave up. She believed in me even when I was suicidal and gave me a sense of being loved, no matter how bad things got for me or how badly I treated her."

I did believe in her, but that would never have been enough. It took three years of medical and psychiatric help to re-tune her body and mind. It took the unceasing patience and gentle help of Paul, the boy who loved her and is now her husband. It also took Becky's own courage and tenacity and inner strength.

This story, from our two points of view, recounts Becky's slide into illness and the long struggle toward wellness. This is a story of desperation, anger, and love—and one of hope.

—*Emma Lou Thayne*

Becky at five months with her mother

CHAPTER 1

Beginnings

I Remember

My husband, Mel, and I have lived in Salt Lake City, Utah, for most of our married life. Though he has a master's degree in history from Stanford University, he has been a real estate broker for forty years. I was a part-time teacher of English at the University of Utah for thirty years. I am now a writer and speak at conferences and workshops around the country. As young parents, we had five daughters under ten: Becky, Rinda, Shelley, Dinny, and Megan.

Becky was our firstborn. From my first hungry look at her, she seemed remarkably beautiful—that new little face, perfect, miniature, with a mohawk of black hair on a head not misshapen even after my forty-eight hours of labor. And she was not crying—only looking around, bewildered. Her tiny mouth sucked curiously on its lower lip, and her not-quite-seven-pound body sat unrigidly in the doctor's palm.

Her father and I had both wanted a girl but had not admitted it. During my five days in the hospital, I lived for Becky's being brought to me because she made me as profoundly happy as I could ever remember being. Not a visit passed that I didn't undress her and marvel, smile, kiss her head to toe, rub my cheek against her unbelievable softness, feel her nuzzle into my neck looking for her dinner. Every finger and toe, earlobe and elbow was silky, the smell of her scalp pure newborn.

Mel could hardly wait to have her home, slicking up our little tract house with its pink nursery, a three-generation cradle, a layette collected ever since we'd been married a year and a half before, a changing table that folded down over a rubber bathtub, and a wicker rocker from the Deseret Industries thrift store that I'd painted white to rock her in. No baby ever arrived more welcome—or more difficult.

Becky was active and bright and adorable. She rolled over at three months but never crawled. She pulled herself up to anything handy and scooted off, walking before she was nine months old. Petite, perky, her fine features almost Dresden-like, she took on the world with little pause for cuddling or even sleep. I watched with amazement as babies of friends slept in church or took naps even with lots of noise around. The rocking I had so looked forward to, Becky would tolerate for only a minute. Then she would be reaching for something around my neck or across the room.

Unprepared, well-meaning, and loving parents of a first child, we made many mistakes. So much came naturally; so much we had to learn. Becky was to be point guard for four younger sisters and, like most oldest children, a beloved experiment for two well-intended but naive parents.

Sometimes we took her for a ride, often on Sundays to have dinner with her grandparents in Ogden, forty miles away. Others had told us that the car motion would lull her to sleep, but it was not until we had another baby, who *liked* the ride, that we realized that the slightest motion made Becky violently ill.

It took time on our part, and misery on hers, to learn about her car sickness, which was common, and how to help.

Years later, it would take a new kind of caring to learn how to help with another sickness so uncommon at the time that it almost claimed her life and destroyed my confidence in how to bring comfort or hope to a child.

I Remember

I remember being a happy little girl. I loved sitting at the kitchen table cutting pictures out of magazines and pasting them into a scrapbook. Creating paper dolls and calendars was my favorite thing. I enjoyed doing things very quickly, and if something took a long time or was tedious, I would simply not do it. When I was seven, I began piano lessons and caught on very easily, sight-reading all kinds of music. It was only for a recital that I perfected anything. Otherwise, I just wanted to play it quickly. My family joked that I played "The Minute Waltz" in thirty seconds.

I had friends who came and went, but my best friend, Debbie, and I did most things together. We had a lot of fun playing tennis and hiking at our family cabin. We never quarreled, and even now, over thirty years later, we're best friends and understand each other in a sort of silent communication.

My mother always expected my sisters and me to help at home, and I liked cooking better than anything else I did around the house. I could be fast at it, and I loved using my children's *Betty Crocker Cookbook*. Potatoes Anna and meat loaf were my specialties, and my favorites were desserts topped with ice cream.

From the time I was about nine, I wanted to be thinner. I guess I was a well-proportioned little girl, except for my waist. It bothered me so much that my tummy poked out. In fifth grade, I remember some boys calling me "fat"

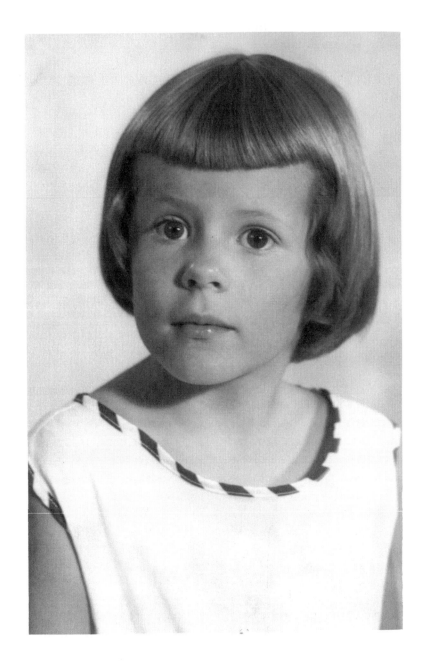

Becky, five years old

behind my back. This made me hurt so much that I focused on going on a diet that lasted on and off for more than ten years.

Besides, my sister, who was eighteen months younger and two years behind me in school, was skinny and could eat anything without gaining weight. The clothes styles we shared were flattering to my skinny sister but not to me. My three younger sisters were still too young to be concerned about weight, but they seemed to grow up thinner than I thought I was.

From the first, I felt angry denial of what I enjoyed. At Sunday dinners I remember thinking I'd better not eat the rolls or the potatoes and gravy—any of the things I liked so much—so that I could lose weight. But then, after everyone was out of the kitchen, I would stand at the counter or fridge and secretly eat more than I would have eaten at the table.

By the time I was thirteen, I was obsessed by the way my body looked. Though many people, including my parents, said I was beautiful, I never thought so. I just felt chubby. In high school I got into Safety Club, Pep Club, Senior Debs, and everything else I tried out for. My grades, especially in English, were good to high, and I graduated with a 3.7 GPA [grade point average]. I went out with the popular boys. I had a group of friends who were close and enjoyed each other a lot. Yet my self-esteem was so low that I couldn't escape my negative feelings about myself. And it all had to do with my weight.

Diet and Departure

In high school all the girls wanted to be thin and were on diets, on and off, all the time. We'd get together on a weekend and make rich caramel corn, and four of us would eat a huge bowl while we talked and laughed. Mostly we talked about boys and dates and how we wanted to be thin for the next dance so that we could wear a small dress size.

I remember the girls in dance club would starve themselves so they would look good in a leotard, and then they'd gain back all the weight as soon as the dance concert was over. One of my boyfriends was a wrestler, and he was always talking about meeting the requirement for the weight he wrestled at, which was ten or fifteen pounds less than he usually weighed. He would run six miles every day before a meet and then use the steam room and sauna to sweat off pounds. The important thing was to lose water weight, so the whole team would starve and not drink anything for a couple of days—and then some of them would not be strong enough to win a match.

Nobody could have told us that we were harming our bodies by doing this. I remember that just before my period I would wake up feeling puffy and gross, and I would make up an excuse for not going to school. I felt very self-conscious when I had to walk past a group of the popular boys who always sat on the steps in the front hall before school started. They made jokes about everyone and laughed, and I felt paranoid and would imagine things they'd say about me. I'd let it build up in my mind. I hated that there was no way to avoid passing them every morning on the way to class.

I remember feeling so much better just by losing four pounds after my period, thinking everyone noticed, when actually no one could see any difference whatsoever. And I never felt okay in front of those boys.

I remember looking at one girl cheerleader's body and thinking, "Why couldn't I have a body like that?" She was so petite and lithe and full of energy. I never felt really energetic because I had not yet found the right sport, which for me now is swimming. In the late '60s, fitness and exercise were not part of our lives, and since there was no pool in our high school, I never learned to enjoy swimming as something to keep me in shape.

None of my friends had cars of their own, but we'd get

to bring the family cars to school sometimes, and we'd go driving together after school and end up at somebody's house, where we'd inevitably eat. On our way there we'd pick up french fries or sandwiches. The mother of one of our friends had her fridge packed with ice cream and toppings and nuts for sundaes or malts. No wonder we all felt the need to diet when we wanted to look better for something special. I just had to find the formula for getting thin and staying there.

The summer after my high school graduation, I starved myself down to 105 pounds after weighing around 120 ever since ninth grade. I would eat only breakfast and then nothing the rest of the day, despite the urgings of my mother. At 5'4", I was short enough so that every pound showed. I got so many compliments on my looks that I felt gorgeous.

HER MOTHER'S STORY:
Diet and Departure

Dieting. That became the theme of night after night of talk—at the dinner table or at any get-together. And then it was about the loss of Becky as a functional member of the family. As a little girl, she had been the leader on our hikes, the organizer of family-night programs, the first up in the morning to practice the piano without any urging. Even as a two-year-old, she would wake up in the nursery she shared with her baby sister Rinda, pull back the curtain over her crib, and say, "Pretty day!" I couldn't hug her hard enough. She loved to ride a horse or swing a tennis racket, and she literally dived into water sports in the summer.

When Becky was in first grade, we moved in mid-year. She had been at the top of her class in reading at a school in an older neighborhood, but in her new school she took an instant dislike to a teacher who almost immediately wanted to change her from left-handed to right-handed, which, on my own instincts and the advice of our pediatrician, we refused to allow.

Though she was behind at the beginning, within weeks Becky had caught up with her class and was doing well. By sixth grade, her teacher told me she was "a genius," that she could write a story better than any student she could remember. We both smiled at her affectionate exaggeration and felt good about Becky.

From fifth grade on, boys were at our door. Becky attracted them as naturally as she returned their attention. With five daughters then under ten, her dad and I felt concern that she set a good example for her younger sisters and grow up to be the "lady" that her grandmother wanted all of them to be.

When Becky was six and her younger sisters nearly five and three, we built a new home that included a wing for my mother. My father had died three years earlier. A profoundly loving but genteelly traditional part of our household, Mother was sometimes bewildered by all of our comings and goings. We were all involved with each other but also involved away from home. Mel was a real estate broker and teacher, away sometimes four or five nights a week. He was president of our church Sunday school and so busy that he seldom noticed Becky's absence except when he wanted to do things as a family, especially on vacations. A bright, good, kind man, no one could have been more interested in doing things "right"—a great believer in hard work, honesty, and conformity.

Three days a week, for one hour each day, I was teaching a class in freshman English at the university, something my girls had seemed to like to hear about when they were younger and grew to respect when they got older. They resented much more my work on the general board of the Young Women's Mutual Improvement Association for our church, which took entire days and nights, writing and editing manuals and preparing for conferences. I tried to take the girls, one at a time, on my bimonthly trips around the country, and we had great times. One trip to

San Francisco, when Becky was thirteen, she "loved more than any trip ever."

When dieting began to rule her life and influence her disposition, I felt her withdrawal from the family and longed to return to the days of her childhood when, for a lovely week at a time, we would be at the cabin—totally "us," all of us hiking, making moss villages, having "alone time." Becky wrote poems like "The Heart of the Canyon." Even as a nine-year-old, life was two-edged for her.

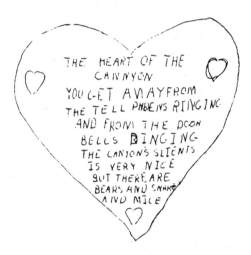

By the time she was thirteen, Becky's differences from her sisters and her indifference to them were most apparent when we were all together, as on family trips. Becky became semi-slovenly in her care of herself, washing her face only to her chin, wearing dingy clothes. Her attention to finishing anything well was haphazard at best, and she argued with me and her sisters about doing any jobs around the house. She and her dad were at swords' points at the dinner table as she became more and more belligerent in her reactions to his suggestions about everything from using too much salt to going to church.

"Mut," Becky's baby name for her grandmother—and one that had stuck—had been Becky's pal even before she became a part of our household. Staunchly independent, driving her own car until the week of her fatal heart attack at age seventy-six, she was important to all twenty-four of her grandchildren. But her influence on our five girls—especially on Becky, the oldest—was incalculable. Of an age when isolation was more threatening than it might have been to a younger person, Mut felt it perhaps more than any of us when, in her midteens, Becky began to move away from family involvement and affection. That pain shows in Mut's letter that accompanied a check for Becky's seventeenth birthday on August 9, 1968:

Dear "Becky"—

It doesn't seem possible that two people who used to be so close could have grown so far apart.

I still have such a tender spot in my heart for you, Becky, and think of so many things I'd like to do for you.

I had hoped to take you and Debbie and her grandmother to lunch. But I knew that would be no fun for you.

So, since money and what it can buy is the only thing you love, please use this for something that will make you happy, and have a Happy Birthday and many happy years ahead.

My love to you,
Your Grandmother

While much of their distance was just the natural coming of age in a young girl wanting her independence, conflicting with a grandmother's demands that the young woman be a perfect young lady, Becky's rejection of Mut was part of the pattern that caused constant tension and instability at home.

Another painful aspect for me was Becky's absence from her sisters' lives. After Becky started junior high, her sisters became a blank in her view of the world, except when we were all on the boat or vacationing at the beach. And they were so engrossed in their own friends and activities that Becky's whereabouts never seemed to puzzle them.

During her high school years, Becky naturally became absorbed in friends, especially boyfriends, and was in and out of the house like a butterfly over a rain swamp. Meals were abandoned in the interest of whatever the current diet demanded. And once she and her friends got drivers' licenses, she was off to school activities and her sometimes job, immersed in the excitement and fears of finding herself almost grown up. But she ignored her sisters and aggravated them with her snubs.

I liked Becky's friends. They spent time in our home, talking, sometimes planning for school, and almost always laughing. It was fun to have her boyfriends there too. Once when my car was out of commission, one of them even took me on his motorcycle—both of us laughing—to the university to teach my class in freshman English. This boy became more important than others to Becky. When he began to swing back and forth between Becky and her best friend, it triggered the alarm that turned into panic as Becky felt anew that weight was the sole index to her appearance and popularity. She withdrew even further.

In general, Becky lived a life apart. She preferred a sleeping bag on the couch in the playroom to her own bed in her own room, the only bedroom not shared with a sister. Our talks began and ended later and later, often not without stormy words when talking about dieting. To me, she was beautiful, anything but fat, and full of abandoned potential. And I knew, of course, that she was desperately unhappy.

Except for Rinda and Dinny, second and fourth daughters, who were naturally thin, one or two of us in the household were *always* trying to lose a few pounds, but this seemed more funny than serious most of the time. I

always claimed I'd lost thousands—the same four pounds every week for years. Megan, then ten, wrote a funny poem about it:

The Dieters

"Tomorrow"
says Shelly,
eating a 4 inch pie from Marie Calendars,
and waste baskets full to the brim of Becky's diet cans.
And Mom,
sneaking a cookie, and thinking Oh it won't hurt,
And then the next day, she's in a bad mood,
cause she got on the scales that morning.
But sometimes *they lose weight,*
and that's when Mom's in the best mood.

But for Becky, dieting was never funny.

I was worried as she turned seventeen, then eighteen, baffled by her need to diet in such strenuous ways. But that was not even close to how worried I became in her freshman year of college, when I felt her going under in some deep region I could not begin to fathom.

Above: Becky, age sixteen, with her family.
Becky is second from the left;
her mother is next to her.

Below: Becky in high school

Becky, age eighteen, starting college

CHAPTER 2

College Freshman

The Doughnut

As a freshman at the university, I was in demand for all of the top activities. I was rushed by the sororities I wanted, and fraternity boys were calling left and right. Even if I was starving, I felt wonderful. It was worth anything to stay at that weight. In my first quarter at college my grades were good, but I lost touch with my friends. Except for my job at a fashionable women's dress shop, dates were all I cared about.

I had met a guy, a "charmer," named Brian, who took me out every night for two months. He took me to meet his family in another state, and everything looked promising. I was completely swept off my feet even though I continued to date lots of other guys.

Then, in the winter, everything changed. He left for two years on a mission for the Mormon Church. He didn't write much, and I had a feeling that he was rejecting me. I felt depressed and worthless. The only bright spot in my whole life was weighing 105 pounds.

I remember the first time I threw up. My friends and I were going to a concert, and I had eaten a doughnut before and thought, "I've got to get rid of this or I'll gain." I went to our downstairs bathroom and put my finger down my throat. It was hard to do, but afterward I felt triumphant because I'd gotten to "eat it but not wear it."

I remember weighing myself faithfully every morning; that magic 105 was where I absolutely had to stay. I began eating more and more and throwing up more and more. It still was not like an obsession. I did it maybe two or three times a week and always secretly. No one knew. But I lost interest in school and in my friends. When they would invite me to go somewhere, I always had an excuse.

I had always thought prayer would help me out of hard situations, but now there were no answers even in that. I had resented my father's lengthy prayers and always wanted to pray independently of anyone else. But even seeking God alone didn't work.

My mother and I would talk almost every night, into the early morning, about my depression and what I could do to become my old self again—meet new boys, forget Brian, get involved in something satisfying. She was coaching the university women's tennis team, and Debbie and I were partners. But I didn't care about anything and hardly went to practices. My mind was on negatives. I'd try different things, like applying for jobs that I really didn't want, and then would feel depressed when nothing worked out. Sometimes I even thought of suicide. It seemed like the only way out. But when I would talk about it with my mother, she would somehow convince me that I should wait and see one more day. I had no idea that she was panicky. She would just try to get me to take some tests and find out what I might get interested in. Nobody in those days talked about depression or probably knew anything about it.

During spring quarter, I wanted to sleep constantly. I'd eat and throw up to maintain my weight. I still wished for a letter from Brian, but I never got one. I had this deep hurting. Nothing interested me—even dating was boring. Home was a shelter where I felt hidden. I felt that my mother was the only person in the world that I could talk to. I was unaware of others in the family and of what was going on around me. My mother was someone I could confide in, but only about Brian. My eating was my own secret, and I wanted something that she couldn't give— self-esteem and even a mild sense of joy.

That summer I went to Seattle with three of my best friends from high school, Kathy, Ann, and Carolyn. I wanted to escape these feelings I had and find a new life. The new life I found turned out to be a nightmare.

HER MOTHER'S STORY:

"Where Can I Turn for Peace?"

Becky's freshman year in college began in comparative happiness. She appeared to be doing well despite her radical dieting. But she seemed a bit brittle, as if something was near breaking, and it was impossible to understand what was causing the distance and nervousness that she showed even in her best times.

Like with Brian. It was apparent early on that she had fallen for him as she hadn't for other boys. "Oh, let it be good" was all I could think. "Let it rescue her from the fragility of a life with no depth."

When her relationship with Brian turned into heartbreak, Becky fell into a depression I had no way of understanding, let alone helping. Of course there had to be more to it than a broken romance. Her self-image had been stumbling along for years. But why? And now why this terrifying plunge?

Back there in the middle of it, desperate, all I knew was that we needed help. I talked to my counselor friend, Ramona Adams, Ph.D., at the University of Utah, worried some with Mel, and consulted most with my mother, whose wisdom in emergencies had brought my three brothers and me up expecting that, no matter what, things work out. Not knowing the seriousness of what we were dealing with, I kept flailing about in those murky waters, counting on the only thing I felt I knew anything about—loving.

Being on the general board of the youth organization for the 5-million-member Mormon Church meant traveling, sometimes once a month, to conferences around the country. In June, the conference came to us, to Temple Square in Salt Lake City, where as many as five thousand leaders would gather to be given new manuals, together with programs for the coming year, often in the form of musicals and entertaining instruction. As chairman of the manual-writing committee and member of the committee for sixteen- to eighteen-year-old young women, I spent twenty to thirty hours a week on my board work, much of it at home, writing, editing, and planning. But the work also took me away. That spring, just before I left for another two-day youth conference, I wrote Becky a letter she saved:

    ... *Beck, I see you so much differently than I'm sure you do. I guess you're beautiful to me in ways that you could never understand. When you ask me, How does my skin look? or, Do I look like I've gained weight? I have a hard time because to me those things seem so trivial when compared to your smile or your eyes or your naive intent on something that interests you.*

    Tonight I stood over your bed as you slept, very deeply thank goodness, and touched your cheek and your hand and wanted to hold you like I used to and sing "Over the Rainbow" and have you put in your own "dear" when I paused. If only I could tell you, Becky, how dear you are to me—how you please me with just being here, with being my friend (not just my daughter). If I seem pushy and overly concerned sometimes, please forgive me. You are my little girl grown up, you know, and it's impossible for me to be indifferent to anything you do or feel. One day when you get a daughter of your own (trite!) you may know this feeling—this overwhelming desire to protect ... and help to make happy.

---

*I know too that a big part of that loving is in letting
you go no matter where your going takes you. . . .*

*Do have a good time these next few days taking care of
your littlest sisters and your dad, who need and love you
. . . you thrive on responsibility in my absence. Remember
as you snuggle down in your sleeping bag, Beck, that I'd
love you anywhere, anytime, doing anything. That never
changes. If I get mad at what you do, please know that I
still love you and wish only to help get rid of the why you
do some things. Please help me to help you if I can—but
then I guess the only way that can work is by your helping
yourself—and those around you.*

*I'm aching tonight, Hon, and wishing I weren't
going. . . . Save me some time when I get back. . . . I'll be
anxious to hear how things go under the new regime.*

I love you.
M

What a fumbling, bumbling letter. So full of platitudes,
so untelling of the anguish of feeling so unable. Mothering
had seemed the most natural thing I ever did, and much
of the time the most satisfying. Also, I could lose myself
temporarily in the richness of my own life as well, with
family and friends, delight in the outdoors, learning,
teaching, writing. And usually I could count on the restoration of prayer and the certainty of help beyond myself.
But with Becky's disappearance into the mire of the sickness that was only beginning to plague and control her,
despair became my companion. Even with four other children I adored, I came to know that you're about as happy
as your least happy child.

So absorbed was I that my preoccupation flooded into
everything I did. Despite the great outlet of my general
board work, my friends on the committee I so enjoyed
said I was "never quite there" in anything that was going
on. But faith in a God who continued to come to my rescue

preserved my sense of right in the world and hope for solace for both Becky and me.

For a conclusion to the international June Conference, where 1500 teachers of young women convened in Salt Lake to be instructed, I wrote the words to a hymn on a Saturday morning. I read them on the phone to a friend on the same committee, Joleen Meredith, with whom I had written other songs for the program. She sat at her piano with the phone on her shoulder, and while I read a line at a time, she composed the music for the song that fifteen years later would be part of a new Mormon hymn book.

That spring, whatever else called me—and fortunately much did—I prayed, hoped, calculated that Becky could muster interest in other possibilities that seemed so accessible if she could only reach—like fun with friends, the outdoors, sports, satisfaction in school, finding the joy of being engaged in something beyond oneself. But nothing appealed to her, and I could see the depression deepening. I had Becky take a battery of tests with Ramona, who reported that she was dangerously depressed and needed counseling and probably a whole new setting to make any kind of comeback.

Then came what I thought would be the perfect solution. Becky wanted to go to Seattle with three good, long-time friends and attend the University of Washington summer school. These were high school friends from Salt Lake who had stayed in touch even though in different sororities and activities at the university. And despite Becky's ignoring them so often, they had been stable, fun, loyal, and productive friends to her. Going to Seattle seemed like a chance to start anew in a beautiful place with different challenges and people. It felt like an answer to my prayer.

Where Can I Turn for Peace?

Thoughtfully ♩ = 80-100

1. Where can I turn for peace? Where is my so - lace
2. Where, when my ach-ing grows, Where, when I lan - guish,
3. He an-swers pri-vate-ly, Reach - es my reach - ing

When oth - er sourc-es cease to make me whole?
Where, in my need to know, where can I run?
In my Geth - sem-a - ne, Sav - ior and Friend.

When with a wound-ed heart, an - ger, or mal - ice,
Where is the qui - et hand to calm my an - guish?
Gen - tle the peace he finds for my be - seech - ing.

I draw my - self a - part, Search - ing my soul?
Who, who can un - der-stand? He, on - ly One.
Con - stant he is and kind, Love with-out end.

Text: Emma Lou Thayne, b. 1924. © 1973 LDS
Music: Joleen G. Meredith, b. 1935. © 1973 LDS

John 14:27; 16:33
Hebrews 4:14-16

CHAPTER 3

Seattle Summer

Flying

I remember getting on that plane in June 1970 flying over Portland, and arriving in Seattle feeling freer than I ever had before in my life. I thought, "This is going to be wonderful. I can do whatever I want." It was like Salt Lake and the depression and all those feelings of inadequacy were behind me.

My friends met me at the airport, and we moved into our small dorm rooms in the almost empty fraternity house we had arranged to stay in because it was cheap and close to the campus. We had all planned to enroll in summer school at the University of Washington. Almost immediately we met cute guys, and the ones I was interested in began asking me out. I thought it was because I weighed 105 pounds.

My friends also felt their freedom, so they "bulked up" and gorged and gained a lot of weight, but I was still throwing up what I ate—on the sly, not with them—so I maintained my weight and felt superior for staying thin, because they didn't get asked out nearly as much as I did.

I was so busy dating that I didn't really care about them. In retrospect, I know that I must have alienated them because of this. But they stayed what they called my "forever friends" and later came to my rescue, despite how I treated them.

As it ended up, none of us registered for school; we were too busy playing. There was a gorgeous park where we would go to swim and take lunch. We would go waterskiing with boys and out to dinner together, or shopping around the campus or to the Space Needle or the International Center, where one of my friends worked. I never realized that everything *was* turning around for me, but too far in the opposite direction. I was feeling euphoric and very energetic. I was hyperactive but still as totally self-absorbed as I was when I was depressed. My mood swing was very different from normal, but all I knew was that I felt great.

I had saved $250 for the whole summer from working at that women's clothing store before I left. By the time it ran out, I was irrational enough to think that I could make a lot of money ironing shirts for fraternity boys. But I was not aware of my irrationality. I just kept writing to my father and mother and grandmother using any excuse to beg for more money. They still thought that I was in school, so they sent limited amounts and insisted that I try to find a real job.

HER MOTHER'S STORY:

The Coming Apart

At first Seattle looked like the perfect answer for Becky. Her letters came often and were full of every excitement her "drab" life in the spring had lacked. But before long we began to realize that her time there was not what any of us thought it was going to be. As she left, she had told us that she would much rather go to Seattle than to the beach with the family for a week in July. She was sure she was ready to be thoroughly away and starting a new life for herself. But two weeks after her arrival in Seattle, she wrote home:

6-21-70

Dear Mom, Dad, Mut, & Family,

I went to two of my classes today. I wasn't very excited about either of them. It's going to be so much reading! I need three books for Anthrop. Dad, could you please mail me a check as soon as possible, for my books? Please leave it blank, 'cause I'm not sure which book store I'll get them at. Mom, I hope you found out about that thing, but I really think I wouldn't be able to raise my average much here.

. . . so I started thinking about Newport and got really excited. When we saw this beach, it reminded me of it and I thought of how much I've loved it every year. That's my favorite thing to do, and I've never been happier than I am there. Besides, I really miss the family and would love to be with you for the last time we're going there. I planned to get ahead in school (take quizzes early)—and borrow some money to fly down. I'd have enough to pay for half if I saved a little of what I'd spend on food. I may not have to pay the full $125 for room, so it'd only be about $40 that I'd have to borrow. I'm sure that it wouldn't be any prob with school, since it's just pass-fail.

Most letters were long and included something to each in the family:

Mut— . . . I really miss you and would like to talk to you. How's the cabin? . . .

Rinda—How's tennis? . . . You'd love all the beautiful lakes up here—they're so neat! . . . Could you do me a favor and look up MaryAnn M. (Kay's sister) in Highland's directory? This letter was returned.

Shelley—I hope you're having fun. You'd love all the boats and waterskiing up here . . . they go so much more than the people do there, it's amazing.

Dinny—those tennis lessons really sound fun. Do you see Sheralyn every day at dance? Tell her hi for me . . . Tell her she ought to be up here. Is your hair lighter from the sun?

Meg—I really miss you especially. Have you been taking good care of Bently [our dog]? Does he still chase you all around the backyard?

. . . I'll write again soon. I miss you all, especially when I think about it!

Love, Becky

P.S. Mom—if you could, I'd appreciate your sending my piano sheet music. There's a piano . . .

Much of what Becky said was exactly what a parent would hope to hear from a daughter off on her own: that she was looking openly and finding new ways to think, that she was becoming independent, her own person. Every day she changed, writing about what she was doing in a hodgepodge of detail and generality. Her thoughts seemed scattered even as they appeared optimistic and full of life:

6-23-70

Dear Family,

. . . A lot has happened since I wrote you. I think I have a job as secretary of rush here at the DU House. Anyway, I went to school a couple of days and hated it. I decided that summertime's for fun, and you didn't seem to be pleased with what I was doing either. I'll probably withdraw and have the tuition check sent back to dad. My friends helped talk me out of it. Why do something you can't enjoy?

I've met so many people and learned so much it's amazing! Everyone is so nice and thoughtful, they make me feel guilty 'cause I don't deserve it. There are so many things I've got to work on, but just realizing it and beginning to understand some things is a big step.

I've gone out with a lot of different guys. None of them excited me much until I met this PKS. His dad is in Real Estate and he's an English major! . . .

Summertime has really brightened my attitude about everything. There's so much beauty up here! . . .

. . . I've decided about religion that it's very important. So many people up here have nothing to base their lives on, not even a family. But I think you can appreciate God just as much by reading about Him and enjoying nature than by sitting in church and getting bugged. . . .

You'd be happy to know that I've changed my eating habits considerably. Although they're still kind of weird, I only eat about 1/4 as much as I had been, and I digest it all! I've lost some weight, and it's really worth it—if only just to save on money.

Another change since last letter is I've decided to save up and try to come to Calif. without your help . . . I'll even give up clothes to be able to come. This seems really funny, but I actually feel that I don't know you very well. I know it was because I wasn't interested in anyone but myself, but I'd really like to change it. I can't wait to see everyone again!

Mut— . . . I answered most of your questions on the phone, but yes, there are more different kinds of people than in SLC, which is good. . . . Yes, I listen to a lot of great people . . . but I still believe what I did before I came. It's so fun living where I do. I couldn't be happier!

Mom—I finally got your letter. Thanks so much. I keep think about how funny it was the night before I left— you doing all the work for me, as usual. Lots of times I've thought about the things you told me during our "late talks." There are a million things I'd like to ask you . . . but I've been so busy. I really miss everything about home.

Dad—I was glad to hear about the two sales—that's great! I hope you've still got my remaining $150. I'd really appreciate it if you could make out a check and leave it blank (the name) for $150.00. You wouldn't believe how much aware of spending I've been! You'd be proud.

Thanks for everything. I'll call Sunday at the usual time.

Love,
Becky

Becky seemed to be thinking through all of the past few months and coming to grips in a superficial way with some of what she said had so troubled her. I wanted desperately to believe what I was reading, as her dad did in his busy, quick looks at her letters, but they had a hollow and hyper sound:

I'm running out of envelopes & stamps! (hint)

6-27-70

Dear Mom,

You're so nice I can't stand it. You wouldn't believe how much that $10 helped. It's a Sat. night & I just got through taking a nice hot shower & washing my neck, elbows, & back and covering my legs with lotion and thinking about you. Every time I get in the shower I remember what you kept trying to tell me. Finally it sunk in! That clean feeling is the greatest.

. . . this week was even better than last. I was busy every second, and I feel like I learn more every day. People are so fun & interesting I can't get enough of them. I never go to bed!

I know it was kind of idealistic to think that everything would change once I got up here, but actually it turned out better than I could ever have imagined possible. Just get-

ting to know my good friends again has been so exciting, even though we do have disagreements, and they're finding out maybe a little too much about me. It'll probably take awhile, but I am learning that other people are sensitive to things I do.

Noticing how beautiful everything is is so fun! That book about happiness that you gave me is so uplifting—I just wish I could remember everything in it and apply it.

. . . Life here is so different. It's really fast-moving, and if you're not on the ball you really get left behind. I've really had to wake up.

I'd like to apologize for being such a selfish person. The least I could have done was try to hide it, like most people do. . . .

You wouldn't believe the dates we've gone on! They really entertain you up here. . . .

I can't wait for the family to come up. I've got all these places I want to show you. . . . My friends are so fun! I got in one of those laughing moods with Ann the other night for the first time in ages. It felt so good!

. . . We went out with these nutty guys & told them that Mormons saved kissing for marriage, just to get out of it. They believed it—it was great! We're gonna tell them the truth, though. I'm realizing how much people are aware of the way Mormons act. Maybe it's just that we're sorority girls, but they sure keep an eye on us.

It's sure different to live with negroes (oops, Blacks) . . . most are friendly & cute just like other guys. We've got all types in this house, and so far just good stuff has happened.

I've got to go iron shirts now. We've started a little business. These are our prices—Shirts .15, Pants .20, Sweaters & T-shirts .10. It's a good way to make a fortune.

Right now I'm trying to decide which is more important—money (food, clothes, entertainment) or leisure time to mess around . . .

Hope you're having fun. I miss you as usual. Thanks

again for everything. Will you mail that discount card for United Air Lines? I didn't get it—hope you did.

Love,
Becky

Mel and I talked long and often about the confusion of her letters, but he saw them only as a good sign of good changes, of her being involved in an active, happy, growing time. The other girls were absorbed in their lives and never aware of my concerns. I wanted to keep our life at home as much like it had been as possible, and certainly it was a lot easier to do this with Becky away. Sometimes I talked to my mother—a very wise woman—about the letters, and she agreed that something was awry. I needed desperately to see Becky, to make sure she was all right. The beach could be more than our usual family outing.

BECKY'S STORY:

Restraints in Newport

In July 1970, I went to meet my family at Newport, California, where we rented a small beach house for a week every year. I really wanted to go, but when we got together, all I could do was criticize Salt Lake. I saw great conflicts in the way people lived there as opposed to how the rest of the world lived. The general feeling of repression there and my dad's conservative philosophy bothered me more than it ever had. I was very vocal in telling my family my negative feelings about where and how I grew up. Most mornings my mother and I walked on the beach and had heart-to-heart talks about values. I remember she urged me not to get into anything dangerous. I felt she was trying to protect me from what I wasn't even doing, like having sex or trying drinking or drugs or just partying and getting away from my standards.

Abrasion on the Beach

We had sent Becky money for her flight, and she met us at the beach. She was a thin, blazing stranger. She had nothing good to say about Salt Lake. Even the cabin and lakes that she had loved were nothing compared to what she had found in Washington. After a few hours, she had alienated her sisters and angered her father. I knew she needed desperately to prove that she was okay, that her decision to go away was wise and her time there beneficial. Her obvious struggle for composure and confidence nearly broke my heart.

While the rest of the family went about the usually happy business of being at the beach, Becky and I walked early and late, talking. I tried not to see the almost panicky brightness in her eyes, the way she held the little finger on her left hand stiffly apart when she walked, and her total obliviousness to anyone else, to what was going on around her, even to the beauty of the sky and the ocean. She was oblivious to herself, too. The good grooming that she had written home about had given way to a kind of dim sloth that grayed her skin and left water marks around her jaw. Any activity seemed forced and compulsive. She played tennis sporadically and swam ferociously, body surfing till we had to usher her in after dark. Eating was the only thing that completely absorbed her, and she left the group after meals just as she had begun to do at home in the spring.

When we left her at the Las Vegas airport on our way back to Salt Lake, I watched her toss a candy bar into her huge bag of dishevelment and walk rigidly to the steps of the plane, excited to get back to her new world. I wept. I was not a big weeper, but I thought my heart would break.

Mel and the girls thought she was just totally absorbed in her time away from home and was trying to exert her independence in pretty heavy-handed ways. But I was afraid. Something was very wrong with Becky. And we were sending her off to manage it all by herself.

Manic

Soon everything escalated. I couldn't sleep more than four hours a night, sometimes only two, thinking of all my big plans for the next day. I would wake up at 5:30 in the morning and go waterskiing with boyfriends. In a letter home just before my nineteenth birthday on August 9, I wrote:

I can barely sit down a minute up here. There's no way I'll be some little stay-at-home housewife. Playing the piano has been so fun. I'm entering this mixed doubles tennis tourney this week. Monday I'm going swimming, then out with Jay. Wednesday there's a rush function we're cooking for. Tuesday I've got a tennis date. Mom, that book is so great—I can't wait to get into it. Jay's my favorite. But I've got to be really careful 'cause it could be another shaft when I leave.

During June and July, I was still throwing up, but that decreased because I was too busy to worry about eating. I did worry about what I weighed. Every day I would weigh myself in a robe that weighed exactly one pound, and my friends later told me that they joked behind my back about wanting to put rocks in the pockets to freak me out. I did sometimes get up to 109, but by the end of the summer I didn't pay attention anymore and quit weighing myself.

I felt very antagonistic toward my family. After a couple of weeks back in Seattle, I wrote home:

8/10/70

Dear Dad,

Our idiotic little argument about attending church was so ridiculous I can't stand it. Here's the same conflict we've had ever since I was old enough to realize that church was a waste of time for me. I can honestly say that the meetings I've gotten the very most out of are those that I've gone to on my own, because I thought they'd be beneficial instead of because you made some ultimatum.

. . . I know, Dad, that your way of life is extremely good and commendable. It works very well for you, but that doesn't automatically mean it's gonna be the best way for me. It's so dang [darn] close-minded to believe that all the other people in the world who don't live the way we do can't get where we're gonna get after death. I agree that the church is a good guideline, but I think that's all it needs to be used as, not a way of life.

. . . If you're smart, you'll not mention the Church unless it's to tell me something interesting that you learned or heard or something. I really enjoy those tidbits. Anyway, if that did happen, I'd know I'd become interested on my own. . . . Please UNDERSTAND AND ACCEPT AND DON'T CONDEMN. Let Mom read this. See you soon,

Love,
Becky

These were strong new emotions that were very difficult for me to handle. None of us had any idea what was really happening to me.

HER MOTHER'S STORY:
The Creeping Panic

By July, Becky had been writing letters that skipped to a new subject in every sentence. They became a staccato rapping at any peace or hope I might have mustered. Such a letter came soon after the vacation. Between its lines of hollow assurances about money and resolutions, I could feel Becky's racing thoughts fueling my racing heart:

7-?-70

Dear Mom,

You're so great! If you knew how much I appreciated that letter. I almost began to get back into my old rut, but I really must catch myself. Your letter really helped. I cried in front of my friends, which was a bit embarrassing, but it's stupid to think that way—crying is a great outlet—I want to do it more.

Today I'm plastering my walls with new ideas. Today I'm staying here all day. I'm actually getting satisfaction from vacuuming, straightening [up] & being creative!

The more I think about the trip, the more I liked it. Our family is amazing. What good times we had just driving along in the car. I really learned lots, too—just what I needed. . . . Whenever I think of Promises *[Promises, Promises, a Neil Simon play we saw in Los Angeles while at the beach],* I get happy. I'll never forget that. Every day was so fun down there.

Mom—you must think I'm the biggest fake! When Dad asked me about how much money I had at the airport, I didn't mean to be lying when I said $3.00. I was just thinking of change. Tell him that, too, okay? The $10.00 will be used wisely, I assure you. I can sure use it. . . .

I find out about the job tomorrow. There's a chance I may not get it. If not, I'll just have to do the best I can without new clothes. They're really not that important, as long as you're skinny! I gained 6 lbs. on the trip, so don't feel bad. [I had joked about my putting on a few pounds.] *Losing won't be that hard for either of us though.*

I really wish we'd had longer to talk, too. Seemed like

---

we'd just get into something & get interrupted. Oh, well, sometime we'll get caught up.

Thanks again—I love you, too, although I'll never be able to say it to your face!

Beck

P.S.S. Bob wrote & said he'll come up after summer school (Aug. 5) with this guy who has a Firebird, if I want him to. I could ride home with them, I hope. I'm gonna write him & tell him to come. He's really nice, but I hope he wouldn't think I owed him anything. I'll just be nice back.

I wanted her home—now. I had a bleak feeling that every day away meant something grim and maybe irreversible for her, and I hadn't the foggiest notion how to help. Was it good or wrong to send money? Should I talk about how she seemed to me, so far from herself, from normal—or avoid the obvious and just try to reinforce how much she had to offer? Where could I turn for help? And with her so far away, how could I help anyhow? And I missed her too.

Summer made its usual brilliant way across our lives, and I kept reminding myself that I had four healthy, delightful daughters at home, a good husband, and a comfortable, inviting life with work and friends I loved. But Becky was far away and in deep trouble. How could we get her home?

CHAPTER 4

The Crash

Nineteenth Birthday

During the days before my birthday, on August 9, I began to feel extremely happy. The emotional chaos of manic depression (as I was to learn later) had taken over my life. It never occurred to me that my parents would have reason to worry about me. On August 4, back in Seattle, I had written to my mother:

---

*Please, Mom, I want to be friends. I love you so much—
you really were my best friend all last winter and spring,
when I needed someone so much. All of a sudden I'm bawl-
ing, probably partly 'cause I'm so tired. I feel so much like
a little girl again. Little kids are so neat—they really are
"naturally stoned."*

*By the way, don't worry about wild marijuana parties.
I gave up the idea long ago, and new people I've met don't
touch it. They really are great people. I know you can find
it anywhere with the right attitude, but for some reason*

*Salt Lake and the thought of it really seems stifling to me
right now. I will be ready though.*

*I'll be so excited to see you, but please don't make it
hard. Like that song says: "Parents, teach your children
well . . . don't ever ask them why, 'cause if they told you,
you would die, so just look at them sigh." You've taught
me extremely well, but being the oldest is dang hard, and if
it gets to be too much harder, I don't know what I'll do.*

*Thanks so much for everything. I keep thinking about
your saying "don't undersell yourself." I'm really not now,
and it's good not to be overselling myself either like I was
last year at this time. I've honestly found a happy medium.*

*Love,
Becky*

Between this time and my nineteenth birthday, I fran-
tically ran around making deals and planning ways to
spend money that I didn't have. I avoided my friends
because they kept saying, "Oh, really, Becky," when I
approached them with my wild schemes, like buying a
Porsche or wanting to go flying over Lake Washington on
a kite from water skis.

I was too obsessed with my plans to spend time eating,
so I would just grab something on the run like a blueberry
doughnut or yogurt or an apple. The boys still wanted to
be with me. I guess because I was fun and exciting. I was
always up about everything, as if I were high on something. How could I possibly know it was mostly my own
mind going out of control?

Sometimes I wrote home two or three times a day
trying to describe my activities and my new ideas. I had
a great desire to be perfect. I thought I needed to be to be
accepted by my family and friends. But I also had resent-
ment toward them. Earlier I had written home:

8/3/70

Dear Dad,

. . . I've been reading this really good book. Some of the ideas apply to you an amazingly lot.

There's this part about parents & kids. It says that a lot of parents have an ideal for the kids and they try to mold them to fit what their ideal is. They usually love the ideal more than the kid, which you don't do, but I do think you want me to live up to your ideal, and if I could you'll be pleased. If you'll realize that maybe it won't be possible for me to do it because I'm different from you, then I'll do my best to please you just by being myself and trying, okay? I really didn't thank you enough for the trip. It couldn't have been better. You know how I am about good-bye's. I just get all flustered. My mind was on a million things. I appreciate all you did. Hope it won't hurt you financially!

I really respect you for your opinions. You gave me lots to think about, too. By the way, what's wrong with socialism?

Love,
Becky

See you all about Aug. 30th, probably.

By the time my birthday came, I felt I could do anything. I must have been determined to be perfect in my own way. I wrote home:

Mom—save this. I may need help, but I mean it.

Dear Family—

Here are my 19-yr-old resolutions. Please help me carry them out. (I'm really sincere.)

Take a real interest in others, help them.

Argue as little as possible.
Be happy, do whatever you want, as long as it
   doesn't hurt anyone else.
Don't steal, and lie only when necessary or when
   you must to be tactful.
Don't compare yourself to sisters and friends.
Take every opportunity to improve yourself.
Listen to others, but know what you believe.
Be versatile—don't get hung up on anything.
Get tons of exercise—stay in good shape physically.
Stay up on current events.
Put forth a real effort in school.
Pray every night.
Eat & drink & sleep in moderation.
Think good thoughts—have the right attitude.
Don't let little things get you down.
Relax—stop worrying.

When my friends in Seattle confronted me because they thought something was wrong with me and suggested I should maybe get some help, I got mad and moved out of the house we were staying in together. The fraternity boys I knew next door said sure, I could sleep in my sleeping bag on their couch in the living room. The next day I wrote another letter. My handwriting had deteriorated steadily, and this letter, like several before it, was on the back of a scalloped paper placemat from a restaurant:

Dad—

I've been thinking some more! Aren't you glad? Anyway, do me a favor and have your secretary type my enclosed letter. Put it on your mirror or in your office or something. It'd really be wonderful if it'd sink in by the time I get there.
   Anyway, I wanna tell ya why I liked Getting Straight. *I thought the acting of Elliott Gould & Candice*

Bergen, two beautiful people, was *great. I liked being
made aware of all the conflicts in society today, and really
thinking about them open-mindedly. It* [sic] *kinda scary,
though, cause there are so many! The show in* my *opinion
covered these modern-day conflicts:*

*older generation vs younger
traditional teaching vs new, more liberal teaching
traditional subjects vs new subjects (sex
    education, black understanding)
marriage vs sex without or before marriage
capitalism vs socialism
conservatism vs liberalism
? vs radical thinking
materialism vs non-materialism
men's dominance vs women's rights*

*Anyway, there are many more that I just can't think of
now. Anyway, I thought the show covered 'em & did it
well, although, like mom said, it was* impractical. *It kind
of made me realize that something's gotta happen, and it'll
probably be one of these three things: change, revolution, or
World World III, or maybe the millennium. Dad—I think
our ideas about politics are pretty much the same, although
I don't really have a reason for thinking the way you do
except that you've taught 'em to me.*

I really like forming opinions on things. I read News-
week *regularly now. . . . School (college) really has bene-
fitted me, and I really appreciate your putting me through.*

Thanks again for everything.

Love,
B

I added a P.S. to my sister Shelley, who was sixteen
and had short light brown hair, because I wanted her to
pose as me and line up a job for me; I would not be home
before the deadline for applying at a new restaurant that
was opening:

Shelley . . . You don't know how badly I need money—
I'm $40.00 in the hole. I hope you're sewing lots. I've got
some really good-looking things to trade with you, if you
want to. We really gotta take advantage of all being able to
wear the same size. . . .

Please write back soon, tell me about Bear Lake, tennis
club, etc. Remember—you're Becky Thayne, 19 yrs. old,
and you're gonna get a dark brown fall [hairpiece] soon
and you need that job!

Thanks—
Love,
B

My family sent me gifts for my birthday. Everything I
did was so important to me that I had great feelings of
elation, then guilt over not wanting to go back home. I
wrote elaborately contrived letters explaining why I wanted
to stay longer in Seattle: like I'd probably just regret it once
I got home, or I've met new guys who are really exciting,
and they've planned all this stuff for me to look forward
to, or I'm just not ready to leave. Seattle's the greatest!

I was going on three or four dates every day with different guys. I'd go waterskiing on the lake at 5:30 A.M. with
Wayne and other guys in the fraternity house, then I'd go
play tennis with Dave, and we'd always win. I remember
being ravenous after excercising, so I borrowed money
from the guys I was with to buy food at little markets. I
was so busy that I bought yogurt and crackers, which I
could eat in a hurry. Every day sped by too quickly.

Afternoons I began going to car dealerships and sports
shops and picking out things I wanted to buy, like a yellow
Porsche and a waterskiing kit. My mind began to race with
plans and ideas for elaborate things to buy that were totally
beyond any budget. I even visited houses with a real estate
agent and let him think I could make an offer on a $250,000

Victorian home in the woods. I had no money left from my savings, and since no one seemed to mind lending me fifty cents here and there, I just kept borrowing. I even talked my father into letting me go on food stamps.

In the evenings, guys took me out to dinner at the Spaghetti Factory or down on the wharf. I was in a state of ecstasy. How could I have known that I was gradually losing all grip on reality? As I look back, I will always be grateful that none of those boys took advantage of my innocence and my fragile mental condition.

My feelings became so intense that I always had to write things down and send them to my family. Things were not good with my friends. When they tried to tell me to settle down or that I wasn't making sense, I got very defensive. I kept sleeping at the fraternity house next door on a couch in my sleeping bag. The boys made me feel welcome and seemed like my big brothers.

I was very adamant about not leaving Seattle until I had to go back to school in the fall. Seattle had become my dream. I felt free to learn about the world on my own terms without my family's interference. I was in heaven.

HER MOTHER'S STORY:

Flying to Becky

We talked to Becky on the phone every Sunday night, but because I was so worried, I began to call more often. She was always exuberant, full of all that she was doing and anxious to tell about it. When she began telling of "a guy who wants to put me through college for ironing his shirts" and that "these guys tell me I can't afford to keep up a Porsche, but I know I can," I knew that we definitely needed help. She sounded as if she were on a dozen pep pills. Was it drugs? Drinking? She had never seemed given to such escapes, but what had happened to her? Had someone slipped her something?

I tried to call when I could talk to one of her friends, but I never found them at home. I had no idea that Becky had moved. Finally, after she called home on a Thursday to ask her grandmother for a loan to buy the Porsche, I got on the phone to ask her what she was thinking. She told me that she was so happy, that she could do anything, that she was the best water-skier in the country, that I should come up and watch her. I asked her how she had improved so much, and she answered that Jesus helped her, that he helped her with everything, that he made her a healer, too.

Becky had never been self-aggrandizing, let alone a braggart, and zealot was the furthest thing from her personality. She told of looking at houses to buy and that the boys at the fraternity house called her "the legend." I hung up sick with anxiety. Whom to talk to? Ramona? All along, Ramona had been a resource, but even she had never recommended professional help—only a change in circumstances, like Becky's going to Seattle. My brother? His was a cocoon world of heart and computer research—and of denial of any problem that couldn't be worked out if one were of a mind to handle it.

And in 1970, who ever thought of depression as systemic? Who had ever heard of "manic"? We still lived in the Dark Ages of recognition, let alone treatment, of mental illness. Ignorance and stigma shoved even the thought of real derangement into some fearful corner too obscure to look at. It would take nearly twenty years for Becky to recover from the shame and bewilderment that swept her for seventeen years into wanting to hide even the mention of what had happened to her. I was not ashamed, but I was bewildered. I knew we needed help and needed it desperately. Still, I hadn't the slightest idea where to turn—except to prayer and action, my all too inadequate responses that had always before come to my rescue.

Saturday night, August 22, I finally reached Kathy, one of Becky's friends, on the phone. She, Carolyn, and Ann had been camping, but Becky had refused to go. Kathy said, "Oh, Mrs. Thayne, something is wrong with Becky." She sounded as anguished as I felt. I called Ramona and described Becky's behavior. She said that Becky sounded as if she had had a manic-depressive breakdown and definitely needed to be brought home for treatment. Within two hours, I was on the midnight flight to Seattle. Kathy said she would try to find Becky—the girls had not seen her in days—and meet me at the airport.

As concerned as he was, Mel felt there was no need for both of us to go, so I flew there alone, writing in a notebook about what Seattle had been to me in my youth—the site of tennis trips when I was a girl. There was Lake Washington to swim in and the beautiful Seattle Tennis Club courts to play on in tournaments and to watch Pancho Gonzales smash overheads and serves. Here had been—for me—the freedom of girlhood that Becky had found, at about the same age. It had been hard for me to come back to Salt Lake those forty-six years before, to leave the lovely abandon of a tennis trip with my friends. How would it be for Becky to leave her idyll, her escape, and to come back decimated by whatever had taken over her psyche and life? I never had been more afraid for what was to come, nor more empty of hope.

What followed was like a thriller movie script. Kathy met me at the airport. There was still no word of where Becky was. For two hours, from 1 A.M. to 3 A.M., we talked with the fraternity boys next door. They obviously liked Becky and were worried about her, but they were totally bewildered. We all decided that indeed she had had a psychotic breakdown and that she needed help, at home. But how were we to find her? Some of the boys had seen her during the day and thought she was on a date with J.

Just after 3 A.M., Becky did come in with him, laughing, delighted to see me, never even questioning why I was there. "Good," she said, "now you can see me waterski and drive my Porsche." Becky returned my hug perfunctorily, needing to tell the six of us all about her shopping spree during the day. She had been all over Seattle bargaining for clothes, sports supplies, other cars, and that house. And doing all this in bare feet that were bleeding and raw from walking barefoot on hot pavement. She carried her sandals, oblivious to pain, her brown, thin, still-lovely legs constantly on the move. She wore tan shorts I had never seen and a scooped-neck, sleeveless top. She tossed her brown hair, slightly disheveled, and gestured with long, unwashed fingers to make her urgent points. Becky had a lost, almost frantic look. Even in our abject ignorance, no one had any doubt that she had left us.

I persuaded Becky to come to her old room, where she could sleep in the upper bunk and I in the lower. I knew I had to keep her close to me. She refused a shower, saying she had things to do. Oh, how I wanted to put those sore, sore feet in a healing soak and rub her head. But it was all I could do to persuade her to lie on the bunk, still in her clothes, to rest.

In the meantime, the boys and I had planned that we would go waterskiing at 5:30 in the morning, as Becky did every day, from the dock on the lake near where some friends of ours, the Cooneys, lived. While Becky skied, I would call a doctor from the Cooneys' house. Perhaps I'd be able to get some medication for her, at least some advice, I hoped, and then get her on a plane home. The girls would pack Becky's things for us to pick up on our way to the airport.

It turned out to be not that simple. Becky did not sleep at all. I woke up after an hour to find her bunk empty. Panicking, I searched the house and found her in the bathroom down the hall, completing an elaborate plan for the house she was buying. In this plan, each of the twenty-five bedrooms became a "shop" named for one of her sisters, or was called a name in rhyme or alliteration: for example, a boutique of diet foods, "The Skinny Dinny"; a spice shop, "The Nut Meg"; "Mel's Belles"; "Mut's Hut"; "Cute Boot"; "Robe Room." On the following pages of this plan, Becky listed items to be sold—her price, their price, and the profit carefully figured. Her brain must have been revved up to megacycles I could not even imagine, with every dormant molecule of originality and creativity spinning in deafening speed in her brain. It would not be easy to direct her *anywhere*.

We did go water-skiing, but she wanted me along and would not hear of my staying on the dock. And she did ski well, even jumping the wake on her slalom, but with a ferocity totally alien to her grinning pleasure behind our boat. Becky wanted me to ski, but I said I needed to go to our friends' house to visit. But when I started up the hill to their place, she came with me. I told her that she needed to fly home with me, that her dad was in the hospital with high blood pressure and needed her—anything to get her on that plane. But she said she wouldn't need the plane, that she could be there faster on her kite, and that as soon as he saw her, he would be healed.

Our friends were out of town, but their daughter, Shauna, and her medical-student boyfriend did everything to help. I dodged from room to room, trying to make a call to the doctor the young man recommended, with Becky too close every time for any privacy. She played "Close to You" and "The Snow Bird" on the piano and cried. She looked at the Sunday paper, saw a picture of a beautiful bather on a beach lolling in the sun with her long hair hanging back, and said it was a photograph of her, that the photographer had taken the picture the day before. Laughing, she cut it out, saying she would take it home to show everyone.

Then Becky began to get angry. She said she would not leave Seattle. In a blurt of language I'd never heard her use before, she stormed out the door, running, and somehow disappeared. We all hunted for her and finally found her going back to the dock. Wayne, one of the young men, persuaded her to come with him by telling her, as we had planned, that he had hurt his back waterskiing and would have to see a doctor.

Never had I felt so desperate. Becky was getting more

distant and irrational by the minute. There was no mistaking the danger. This was not an idiosyncratic or even neurotic episode. This was something I had never seen before, a complete mental breakdown and a fearsome emergency. Oh, Becky, I thought, where have you gone? How will you find your way back?

I had to keep my composure, not let her suspect what was really going on. But I felt like wailing, as if we were all part of some Greek drama that couldn't be real. More than anything, I knew we needed help—fast.

BECKY'S STORY:

Yielding

I vaguely remember seeing my mother when I came in that night in Seattle, and thinking, "Oh, I've got to show her what a good water-skier I am." I was so proud of myself for being good, and I needed to show off. I wanted her to meet J, because he was the one I was really interested in, and I thought he was so handsome. But when I saw everyone in that upstairs room, I vaguely felt that they were all against me. Still, I didn't care because I felt so euphoric.

When my mother wanted me to go to sleep, I remember thinking there was no way I could. I had too many important things to plan. Everything about what I did is unclear, but I do remember something about the list for the house and the alliteration of the names for the rooms. I remember that my mother pointed out the blisters on my feet, but I thought it was kind of funny. Maybe I was into hurting myself subconsciously for attention. I felt radiant, probably because I was thin and because I had so much ego-boosting attention from boys everywhere.

The next morning, I remember thinking that I could fly home on my kite and that I could walk on water, that I was enlightened, and that I had some sort of spiritual power. I remember being in our friends' living room, playing the piano, and laughing and then crying and not being able to stop. No matter what I did, I couldn't control my emotions on my own. It was a strange feeling, but I still thought I was okay, and no one could have told me that I wasn't okay.

In my euphoria, I didn't suspect that my mother was there to put an end to all my fun. But when we got into the car to go to the doctor, supposedly for Wayne, I began to think she had tricked me.

Walking into the doctor's office at the community hospital, I began thinking, okay, I'll see the doctor and go along with what they're doing. I think at that point I was starting to realize that I was not all right, probably because of the way Wayne and Mom were urgently trying to get me help. I sensed something, enough so that when I saw the doctor, I finally just decided to give in.

I remember feeling a great sense of giving in and thinking I needed something to relax me. This was really the turning point of my summer—to give my arm to the doctor as if to say, "Help me, I need help." It was like a huge break in the momentum, as if I had hit bottom. It was almost as if I had lost consciousness and was ready for a new life.

HER MOTHER'S STORY:
Airport and Flight

It seemed as if the doctor was with Becky for only a moment when he called me outside to say that she needed immediate hospitalization. When I pleaded with him to let me take her home, he said that he could give her a shot that would take effect in twenty minutes. At that time, she would go into a deep sleep, so we would have to be on the plane before that happened. The airport was over half an hour away, but we thought we could make it. One of the boys, Dave, said he worked at the airport and knew a shortcut. The girls at the dorm could ship our bags and clothes home.

I felt as Becky must have felt in the night, wound up for action. Fortunately, I thought to ask the doctor for a note permitting us to fly with Becky under the influence of a drug. I called the airline to ask the cost of the flight so that I could have a check all made out for the tickets I ordered. I called Mel at home and my brother, a doctor, and they said they would have a psychiatrist with them to meet us.

Then we were in the car and Dave was going up to 120 miles an hour on the freeway. Becky and I were in the backseat, and she was getting angrier and angrier at me for suggesting the flight home. She said she could cure her dad, that she would get out of the car right then and send vibes to make him well. I knew she would never be persuaded to get on that plane.

But then we were there, that is, almost there. Just outside of the airport was a traffic jam, monumental in the rubble of renovations. Dave had to stop. I said, "Becky, remember how you love to beat me in a race? Well, I'll race you to our gate—C5." She was out of the car and we were both running, she still in bare feet, both of us in shorts, tearing through traffic and the crowds.

We reached gate C5. (There was no security check in 1970.) I stopped at the counter and said I was the person who had called. Our tickets were made out, I handed the attendant my check, and we flew to the sliding glass door that was just being closed. We must have looked as desperate as I felt, because someone opened the door and we ran to the metal steps that were being pulled away from the plane. Again, somehow something convinced someone to let us go up the stairs. But a flight attendant met us at the top and said, "You can't come aboard in bare feet."

I handed her the note from the doctor, and she called the pilot, who came out and read—on stationery from Overlake Memorial Hospital—this note I saved:

To United Air Lines—

Miss Becky Thayne has my permission to travel with her mother to Salt Lake City. I expect no untoward effects.

RDA [name changed], M.D.

The pilot waved us on. We barely made it to the front row of first class before Becky was asleep. The flight attendant and I strapped her into her seat belt, and I tried to make her comfortable with a pillow against the window. She slept soundly for just over an hour.

I watched her sleeping and prayed that she would not wake up until Salt Lake. And for the first time in my life, I wished ardently that something would happen to the plane, that we'd go down, so she would not have to face the pain of the life that seemed inevitable for her. She looked beautiful to me—and childlike, helpless, relaxed for the first time I could remember. All I wanted to do was cry, but I could not afford to do even that.

I talked with the understanding attendant about Becky's condition. Together we planned that when we arrived at the Salt Lake airport, she would usher everyone else off the plane first. Then, when Becky got off, she could meet the doctor without a crowd to contend with.

Suddenly, Becky was awake, thumbing through the Sunday paper she had brought, pointing to the picture she thought was of herself, saying, "Mom, all I have to do is send this to Brian, and he'll be able to convert anyone." She asked for a pen to label it and give instructions. I tried to keep her talking about it, about anything, but she spotted the trays going by for lunch and called to the attendant for one—then another. She ate everything on her tray and mine, then from the extra tray, and asked for more.

I tried to get her to take the pills the doctor had given me in case she woke too soon. But of course she refused,

saying she didn't need anything but a chance to see Brian—
and some more to eat. By then, Salt Lake sounded like a
giant rescue, but also the beginning of an end that I
dreaded. How would this nightmare end? My skin rum-
pled about me, and I felt as lost as Becky.

We landed. As planned, everyone else got off, the
attendant having told Becky they wanted to let her off last
since she had been the last to get on.

Becky did not even question why her dad was there
waiting with her uncle and a psychiatrist we all knew from
our neighborhood. Off the four of them went, headed for
the hospital. I was sure Becky would be pleased to get rid
of me, her tormentor, who had interrupted all that she
could possibly have longed for in a summer in Seattle.

Years later, I would write what I never could have
expressed then:

For My Child in Pain

I would curl you back into my womb,
monitor what we ate, drank, injected,
how we slept. I would move us back further,
past conception, call on configurations
of genes, move this one, that one
by imploring the Power I never deserved.

I would offer my maidenhead,
my sight, my fingers, the sound
of my streams.

I would return myself
to facing my knees in that other womb
asking my mother's rich waters to issue me
newly permitted to bear you,
to give the unspeakable joy of the bearing,
the having, the letting go, the holding
to you.

You would be safe. And we
would be born again, free. *

Landing

I don't remember getting to the plane or running to catch it; I only remember wanting to sleep. I was in a state of doing what I felt like, which was eating and not caring. My body was like lead. I must have been so tired from lack of sleep for weeks and then going at a pace that was way too fast that this resignation felt wonderful to me.

The whole trip is cloudy, but I do remember seeing my uncle, who is a doctor, as I got off the plane. I was glad he was there. I didn't even notice my dad or wonder why my mother didn't come with us. I just had a feeling of being taken care of and that I was incapable of making decisions. I didn't even think of Seattle or that that part of my life was over. There was the sense of being nobody and coming from a whole different place. I felt numb; that was all. Months later, I would look back on Seattle as a dream world where all my fantasies had become real.

* *Things Happen: Poems of Survival*, Salt Lake City, Utah: Signature Books, 1991, p. 25.

CHAPTER 5

Intermittent Hospitalization:

August–November 1970

BECKY'S STORY:

The Hospital and Paul

I don't remember much about being in the first hospital except that I wanted to sleep. I looked forward to meals and didn't care about anything. My eating was out of control; I was even eating off other people's trays in a room on the psychiatric floor where we all ate together. I learned later that the medicines I was taking—lithium and Thorazine, Stelazine, or Mellaril—stimulated my appetite. I heard all of the names, but had no idea what they did, only that I felt heavy all over and was always starving.

I resisted taking the drugs because I hated how I felt. I would act as if I had swallowed the pill, but I had really just put it under my tongue. Then I would spit it out. I felt somewhat antagonistic toward the doctor because I didn't understand what had happened to me. It seemed that no one told me anything. I just wanted to get away from that horrible place.

In the three weeks that I was there, I saw nightmarish things, such as a naked man who exposed himself numerous times in a large window I had to walk past to get to the day room. There were a lot of older people in the room who would sit and watch TV and talk gibberish. They seemed scary to me because they didn't make sense when they talked, and they looked crazy. I thought, Why am I here? What did I do wrong to be punished like this? What do I need to do to leave this wretched place?

A big part of my bewilderment and anger was knowing that the door was locked, like a jail, and I couldn't get out. A couple of times I tried to sneak out when visitors were let in with a key, but there were always people watching. I didn't know where I wanted to go; I just wanted to be on the other side.

There was one staff member whom I got to know, and I could talk to him better than to anyone else. He was a nice young guy and seemed to take an interest in me. He even came to visit me after I was out of the hospital, but I was embarrassed and ashamed about where we had met, and I must have discouraged him.

In the hospital, from the first, I thought a lot about being married. I thought that would be a way out of this misery, and I remembered a guy named Paul whom I had dated twice before going to Seattle. We had written quite a few letters back and forth when I was in Seattle and he was in the National Guard summer camp at Lackland, Texas. I enjoyed his letters but didn't think much else about him. He was funny and a good writer. For example, he wrote:

Monday, June 1, 1970

Dear Becky,

Thanks for the letter. It was great. You don't realize how helpful & satisfying "words from home" can be in this Inferno. Aside from going home, it's the only thing we Airmen Basic have to look forward to. . . .

I wrote this Alfred Hitchcock poem, guaranteed to chill your bones.

Basic Blues—Edgar Allan Markosian

Branded body of khaki green
Once human, now machine,
Breathing air yet succumbed heart
Conscience numbed by a graveled bark.

Mailed from life a fortnight ago
Mothballed his "civys" & self & soul
Away from taste, from walking free
Now "marching in time" to eternity.

Entangled, trapped in military twine
Kiss the Big Man, rank and climb
Chanting cancer, "all be like me"
To clothe and spread conformity.

Oh Army eye, see paradise there
In marching rows of shaven hair
"By the book"—where all beauty lies
As in rows of headstones, nicely organized.

. . . Good luck at Washington.

Love,

25 days 'til freedom!

Paul [his own cartoon with shaved head]

Sometimes he wrote on a music staff, to notes, like "Hel-lo Becky it's Sunday afternoon and I'm writing a letter to you yah yah." He was always original, like:

The only thing that keeps you awake is the "Instructor's" colorful language—a tape a' one of our previous classes would've put Who's Afraid of Virginia Woolf *to shame. . . . I was wondering if you would mind sending*

me a picture of a nice racket—with you holding it. P.S.
That tennis racket doesn't really have to be too noticeable.

I don't remember calling Paul from the hospital, but he said I did, and he came. Later he wrote a short story about how excited he was as he drove up to see me in the rain in his Volkswagen. He said the windshield wipers kept saying to him, "Becky Thayne, Becky Thayne." It was a total surprise to him to find me in the psychiatric ward. I remember lying on the couch in the day room, asleep, and having an attendant wake me, saying, "Becky, you have a visitor." I looked up, and there was Paul, smiling. He looked really good. He was tall and thin and tan and very handsome. I was glad to see him, and strangely I was never embarrassed. With him I could be myself—whoever that was.

In the next weeks, he came every day and brought his guitar. We'd go out on the back porch of the hospital, and he would sing and play for me and comfort me. He even helped me compose songs that I thought were great. But at times I wasn't in the mood to be with him, or he would do something that bothered me, like humming, and I'd tell him to leave. Sometimes I was just too tired to give anything to him—or to anyone else at that point.

I don't remember wondering why my family didn't come to visit me. I had no idea that the doctors had told them not to. They had asked that none of them or any of my friends come because, I found out later, I was supposed to start over, with none of them to upset me. So for a couple of weeks, Paul became my only link to the outside world.

When my parents were finally permitted to come, in the third week, I had them bring things I craved such as strawberry instant breakfast and malts. I would show them the little items I had made in the craft room: tile hot plates and painted ceramic dishes. It all felt meaningless to me. It was still a time of numbness, when I didn't look forward to anything and didn't respond in any of the ways that I used to.

I was vaguely angry and must have been paranoid because I thought the hospital personnel were against me. But the hardest thing to realize was that the people on the ward were insane and therefore I must be, too.

Recovery, the Hospital, and Paul

What could there be for Becky now? When the plane landed in Salt Lake, I saw her walk away in bare feet, still holding her sandals, with her dad and uncle and a doctor whom I had to trust like God. Someone had to be able to help her. There had to be a way to let her have her life. I was wrung like a wet chamois to limp nothingness. How to tell the other children, her grandmother? How not to fall apart now that I didn't have to stay together to meet the emergency?

One of my first accesses to any stability was a surprising one. It was finding a definition for what I had seen happen to Becky. Everything had seemed so indefinable and terrifying, as things are when we know nothing about them. Ramona lent me a book containing a clinical definition of manic-depression. It could have been Becky exactly:

mania (ma'ni-a) The term is commonly used today in conjunction with melancholia, *since the two states are regarded as manifestations of a single disorder called manic-depressive psychosis. The principal characteristics of mania are expressed in three fields: of ideas, feelings, and motility. Each of the three shows pronounced exaggeration, in the sense that ideas are voluminous, feelings are intensely elevated, and there is marked psycho-motor overactivity.*

The main disturbances in the ideational sphere are: overproductivity, flight of ideas, *that is, a rapid shift-*

ing from one topic to another of which distractibility is a part, the patient changing from topic to topic in accordance with the stimuli from without and from within; the shifting may be occasioned by what is called clang *association—stimulation of a new train of thought by some external sound;* leveling of ideas, *that is, essentially all topics have about the same value to the patient;* ideas of importance, grandiose ideas, *the patient expressing delusions of greatness perhaps in all fields; the feelings of well-being are expressed also in the sphere of* physical excellence. . . .

The principal modifications in the emotional field are: exaggerated feelings of gaiety, well-being, extreme happiness—in consonance with the ideas expressed.

The expression psycho-motor overactivity *refers to physical overactivity. In extreme states it is incessant throughout the waking hours; the patient attempts to motorize, that is, to put into physical execution all the ideas that occur to him; this tendency, therefore, leads to a shifting of physical activity paralleling that in the mental sphere. . . .*

. . . the content of mania is no different from that of melancholia. . . . Both disorders are wrestling with the same "complex," and in melancholia the ego has succumbed to it, whereas in mania it has mastered the complex or thrust it aside. . . . Mania is not a genuine freedom from depression but rather a cramped denial of dependencies. . . .*

Somehow reading that made me better able to begin to pick up some pieces, as I told the family about my trip to bring Becky back from Seattle. I needed to let them understand her illness, that it was no different than if we'd found she had diabetes. Something was out of balance, and it could take some time before the doctors could determine the best treatment for her. In the meantime, Becky

*Leland E. Hinsie, M.D., and Robert J. Campbell, M.D., *Psychiatric Dictionary* (3rd edition), New York: Oxford University Press, 1960

would have to be in the hospital, where they could treat her most efficiently. It might be a while before we could see her or bring her home. I needed to explain too that the doctor had said Becky was too angry at me for bringing her home and too withdrawn from the rest of her family and friends to respond with anything but indifference or disgust.

In Mother's rooms, where we gathered, those four younger girls looked so precious I thought I would choke with love and agony. My brain spun and my heart crashed in my chest. My body felt as heavy as Becky's had looked getting off the plane. We all had to do whatever we could to make things better for her. But what?

I felt we lived in as happy a home as was the realistic lot of any family. We had fun together, we laughed, we talked, sometimes we argued, but we seldom quarreled. We were in touch. I liked my children as well as loved them, for their differences as well as their alikenesses. They had friends and were busy and hardly ever in trouble. Of course, they were as subject as sisters might be to rivalry and defense of possessions. One put a little padlock on her door when she went to camp with a note that said: "*Nobody* enter! And *no* clothes better be missing!" But most of the time, the girls were friends with each other. That is, until Becky started junior high and began to be a sort of separate entity. Her antagonism toward Rinda was fired by what she saw as Rinda's perfect shape. It was more than apparent that Becky didn't want to have anything to do with Rinda and this was even more true after Becky had been to Seattle.

Rinda, eighteen, and Shelley, sixteen, did a lot together. Sometimes they double-dated, and they often took their youngest sister, Megan, on dates with them. Dinny, twelve, was a pig-tailed perfectionist. Of course, all of them would later acknowledge times of feeling threatened by a sister's talents or appearance, but mostly they were pretty compatible. It wasn't until they were all married that they fully appreciated just what good friends they really were. But for me, in their growing up, they were my dears who graced my days, never left me bored, and challenged me—a lot.

I had shielded them from my moments of panic and despair. I tried to buffer Becky's interactions, tried to allow Becky the space she so obviously wanted without communicating to the others how frantic her withdrawal made me feel. One of the questions that arose, terrifying and insistent in my blacker moments, was: Did I cause this? Did something that I did or failed to do contribute to Becky's illness?

I genuinely loved mothering and felt that we never were really apart even in my professional travels, teaching, or writing. But I was never unaware of the passing of time and the impossibility of holding still at any stage. And no matter how hard I tried, I was forever plagued by the question of Golda Meir, the late Israeli Prime Minister, to herself: "Who or what have I neglected today?" In my first book, my master's thesis, published in 1971, the year after Becky's first hospitalization, was this poem:

Goodnight*

Softly aging here
I move from bed to bed
and measure out my tired time
in lengths along their languid,
covered legs.
Five daughters sleeping to my touch are
spread across the pillows
honeyed to their hair
and take my kiss in ways as
different
as their eyes and ages.

Eight balls up tighter,
nudges me, and sighs.
Fifteen startles wide and then
collapses into quiet recognition,

smiling. Seventeen hardly stirs
but breathes against my cheek some
gentle sound. Twelve tenses, turns,
and pulls me down in fierce acknowledgment.
And nineteen rolls
away to cover up to my brazen tattoo
on her cheek.

I move toward the stairs
vulnerable, divided into fifths,
and come to you
to be made whole.

Such moments of wholeness were rare. As the three weeks of Becky's hospital time dragged by, I was assailed by an agonizing guilt. Had I ever done one thing right in raising any of them—especially Becky? How had I failed? What could I have done differently? What fearful mis-guidance of mine had brought her to this loss of herself and what seemed at the time like the loss of her life? What if we had found help sooner? Why weren't we smarter? Why didn't I do more than just talk with her and try to reason our way through what I knew was a threatening disaster? Not until months later did Rinda, then seven-teen, say to her dad and me, "You know, I've never heard you guys take credit for one thing any of us have done that was great, but when we do anything not so great, it's all your fault!" It was a wonderful thing to hear from a child—and probably true.

But the guilt had a way of hanging on grotesquely to every effort to help with any comeback for Becky. It would be a long time before we would be able to accept the fact that most of her disease was probably hereditary, a chem-ical disorder that was waiting for something to trigger it. What helped the most was finding over weeks, months,

Spaces in the Sage, Salt Lake City, Utah, Parliament Publishers, 1971, p. 6.

even years, that it could be treated with medication and time. But, oh, the pain in the passage. The mixture of the manic-depression and the bulimia and anorexia that were to follow was, in 1970, a foreign world even for doctors.

The Zero Time

When I was in Seattle, I had thought about my sisters in a loving way and was able to appreciate their good qualities. Probably because I was far away from them and also because I was so high from the mania, I loved everyone, strangers as well as friends. Physical involvement with anyone had no appeal for me. I had no desire to be close to anyone even though I did let several of the boys kiss me. There was no depth in any of my relationships. I just felt euphoric.

Ever since junior high, I had really resented Rinda because she was "skinny." I just didn't want to have anything to do with her. But when I was in Seattle, I invited her to come up for my birthday. I showed her around, and for the first time that I could remember, I had a good time with her. She brought presents from the family, and I loved everything, especially a pair of copper-colored Weejuns (shoes) that I wore forever. I said good-bye to her on a very good note.

That would be the last time for years that we would have any real connection.

A lot of what I felt when I was first in the hospital is just fog. I slept a lot, and still thought and dreamed all the time about Seattle. I wasn't concerned with my friends or family. I just existed and was out of touch with reality.

My sessions with the doctor were useless to me. He seemed not to know how to relate to me and would just sit and stare at me. Whenever anyone came to wake me up to do crafts or to be with people, I would resist, but then I'd go and do it, not even halfheartedly. The nurses and doctors just bothered me. I didn't want to have people in my life. During my first stay in the hospital, my family was a total zero to me.

Becky out of Touch

The doctor had told us about lithium, a new drug that might prove virtually miraculous, along with antipsychotic drugs, to treat the acute stage of Becky's illness. The whole thing seemed totally unbelievable. During the first week, I ached to see and hold Becky, but when the doctor permitted visits, our times at the hospital felt futile. Conversation was about nothing that mattered, always far off, and I longed for the talks we used to have. Her dad and I toured her new world of a bedroom, a crafts room, a TV room, and halls, halls, halls, with a dull realization that everything was uneasy, unreal, dimly nightmarish. If it was that way for me, what was it like for her? I sensed her lack of interest in anything but sleeping and eating. Whether I went alone or with Mel, I seldom stayed for long. I came to rely more and more on Paul as our connection to Becky and, outside of the doctors, our hope for her recovery.

Release

I remember the day I got out, three weeks later. My father came and signed papers, and I walked up a steep hill with him to the car. I felt closer to being happy then than I had felt in three weeks, yet I was very afraid of dealing with this outside world. I was almost suicidal, I was so lost. I thought, what now? It was an overwhelming feeling of worthlessness and inadequacy. I had let myself go with my weight and felt fat and ugly and unready to face anyone, let alone my best friends and sisters. I was so despairing that nothing mattered, not even that Paul would be there waiting, too.

A Place for Becky to Live

When Becky came home after three weeks, we tried to make her life as different from the hospital as we could. But there was no "normal." I tried to fix tasty, healthy meals, and she sat with us only long enough to eat, and then she would disappear—we knew now—to throw up. Tension mounted. There was no ignoring the disease; it belonged to all of us.

The following weeks were lived on the alert. Friends I'd known intimately said I faded from view. Totally preoccupied, I spent my days reading about illnesses like Becky's, inquiring of experts, talking to doctors. One week after she came home, she went back into a psychiatric ward from September 17 to October 3. We went through three doctors, all of them despairing at Becky's resistance to medication and her determination to get back to Seattle by any means. One of the doctors told me, "I'd rather treat half a dozen depressives than one manic. They don't want to get well. They like the feeling of thinking they're God."

Finally we were directed to Dr. Bernard Grosser and his insightful treatment of a combination of illnesses as uncommon at the time as they were challenging to overcome. We trusted him from the beginning, even when he said Becky needed to be readmitted after being home only two weeks. Dr. Grosser said she needed to establish a routine so that she could begin to get well. This time— the last time—Becky was hospitalized for thirty-two days. The doctor's clinical diagnosis tells us in retrospect what Becky's condition was:

Becky Thayne was admitted to the psychiatric inpatient unit of the University of Utah Medical Center on October

---

21, 1970. She had been hospitalized from August 22 to September 10, 1970, and from September 17 to October 3, 1970, at a community hospital for a first episode of mania with psychotic features. Although the bipolar disorder was treated appropriately with phenothiazines [Thorazine and Mellaril used in acute phase to control psychosis before lithium can take effect] and lithium, management in the outpatient setting had been difficult because of resistance to taking medication, frequent self-induced vomiting and laxative ingestion in an effort to lose weight. These behaviors made it impossible to adjust lithium dosages adequately and admission to the University Hospital was advised.

On admission, Becky presented as an appropriately dressed, attractive young woman who was obviously uncomfortable at the prospect of a third confinement in less than two months. Some anxiety and agitation were present, but speech was not pressured nor was there evidence of manic excitement. No psychotic thinking was elicited; however, there was some loosening of associations. No evidence of gross cognitive deficit was noted; however, she refused to take some of the tests (e.g. serial 7's). Judgment was noted to be poor and she had no insight into her illness. Pharmacotherapy was initiated using thioridazine and lithium, 1500 mg per day. During the course of hospitalization, she demonstrated herself to be at times a petulant, manipulative, impulsive, and narcissistic young woman who exhibited considerable fluctuations in mood. Many times during the course of hospitalization she was noted to attempt binge eating followed by self-induced vomiting.

She was discharged on the 32nd hospital day on low-dose thioridazine and 900 mg lithium per day. Close follow-up sessions with me and a behavioral therapist were planned to monitor pharmacotherapy and to correct the bulimic behavior. (In addition to the bipolar illness, Becky could be diagnosed under current diagnostic criteria as having anorexia nervosa because of the striving for weight loss of less than 85% of normal weight, and as bulimia nervosa because of the frequent episodes of binge eating and purging.)

11/89
Bernard Grosser, M.D.
Professor and Head of Psychiatry
University of Utah School of
Medicine

The combination of medication and hospitalization was a beginning, but only that. A simple salt, lithium had been accidentally discovered as a treatment for manic-depression in Australia only a few years earlier in experiments on heart patients, who became calm after its use. Before the discovery of lithium, remedies for Becky's symptoms might have been shock treatment and long hospitalization. Now the treatment of lithium combined with imipramine, an antidepressant, meant that Becky's body chemistry could be stabilized, giving her a chance to start her long climb back to normal.

What happened in those next years was all part of the jagged course that any healing process must take. Nothing happened overnight. Nor did we recover easily, any of us. Not only was Dr. Grosser generously on hand for consultation any hour of the day or night during those three desperate years, but he has been a calming influence as well as a great source of reference when we've called to ask questions ever since. He now calls Becky his "star patient."

But in the beginning, none of us felt very starry about anything. Visiting Becky during any of her three hospitalizations was like walking into the hell I knew it was for her. The closeness that we had known all of her life drifted off into some nebulous distance. After one visit, feeling like a nonperson myself, I wrote a poem with no capitals or punctuation, a poem as lifeless as the joyless world that had claimed my daughter:

Visitor on the Ward

Pervasive as glue the acrid smell of the shadow shapes
sloughs through the halls the rooms empty like smoke
as the interred rise to float down the furtive corridors
eclipsing color in their windowless maze taking the air
along soon i cannot breathe waiting i fondle my keys in
my safe pocket then you appear like puffed sleep undipped
in day your muscles have not found themselves even your
smile has forgotten where to go you wear dishevelment like
cotton candy put out to blow i know i know you somewhere
where have you gone is wandering these hallways of
peripatetic clay
the only way to finger animation and as the pills are washed
into the streams where sensibility began what parts of you
are carried off in screams dredged under by your proud
ican youseeican imgoing home

Recovery, the Hospital, and Paul

I was so disappointed both times that I had to go back to the hospital, yet I knew I wasn't well and that I never would be. I had no desire to do anything but eat and sleep. The University Hospital, where I was the third time, though not quite as bleak as LDS Hospital had seemed, was still not a pleasant place to be. I remember waking up in the morning and wanting to go back to bed as soon as possible. I noticed that people were like shadows floating around aimlessly or watching TV game shows all day.

I'd get a pass to go down to the snack shop and get malts, drink them, and then throw up. Sometimes I'd see some pre-med students I knew and I'd want to disappear. More than just embarrassed, I felt scorned because of my looks. I totally hated myself, and since I had no way of understanding what my problem was, I felt all alone. I think I knew I was sick, but I couldn't see past it. I felt too weighed down even to try to deal with an hour from now, let alone tomorrow. I couldn't wait to go back to sleep.

Sleep was the escape I loved. I would have exotic dreams, and I enjoyed being somewhere besides in my troubled world. When a nurse or aide would wake me to get me started on some small project, I'd get very annoyed at being disturbed. There was certainly nothing I wanted to do. I felt ashamed of what I was—a nonentity—yet I had no drive to change my existence. I probably resisted as much as possible, and they would physically draw me into the craft or TV room.

The people at the hospital scared me, except for one girl about my age named Janice. She had red hair and seemed like a very kind person. I felt that we had something in common, being there together. We talked about surface things like boys and high school. She had known Paul in high school and spoke very highly of him, which made me appreciate him more. I felt connected to her somehow, but I wasn't able to care enough to say goodbye when I left.

My two good friends, Debbie and Jan, came to visit one day. That was the first time I'd looked forward to having visitors. I could tell they were shocked when they came, even Debbie, my oldest friend. I knew I looked different, and I felt uncomfortable with them and didn't know what to say. I wasn't the Becky they knew. Later Jan said that my eyes looked blank, and she remembered that that was scary to her.

One day in the snack shop, I saw a man from our neighborhood and asked him to take me home. He had no idea that I shouldn't leave, so he dropped me at my house. It was kind of a feat for me to trick someone into thinking I was normal. I wasn't trying to escape; I just wanted to be home for a while. I don't even remember what anyone said or how long I stayed, only that I had to escape for as long as I could.

86

As the weeks passed, I began to improve my behavior so that I could get out of the hospital. Dr. Grosser would see me often and encourage me to do things to get better, trying different drugs. Like all the other doctors, I thought he was against me, too, so I didn't like him. But I did what he said so that I could get out.

Finally, I responded to lithium. My blood levels were checked day after day and were found to be right. The doctor told me that if my level jumped too high from too much lithium, the effect would be toxic and I could die. It must have scared me enough to submit to the tests. I also took imipramine, and I felt a little better when the antidepressant worked and I was allowed to go home, though I was far from being well.

Paul came regularly, always trying new ideas to help me. I loved hearing his guitar music and always felt comfortable around him. I knew he'd stay with me, and I was glad someone cared. He soothed me with his understanding nature.

I felt distant from the family and tried not to be around them again, especially when I was throwing up.

Recovery at Home

When Becky came home just before Thanksgiving, she was vapid but defiant, determined that she would find a way back to her idyll in Seattle. I watched her drag from upstairs to downstairs, famished, eating everything in sight, her attention span like an infant's, wanting nearly always to sleep. I saw her shuffle one foot in front of the other, her lovely features immobilized, her bright brown eyes dull, the normal appearance of her whole body misshapen by drugs and despair.

That flatness about her was the killer for me. I felt like a blob of tears that couldn't cry. It was all I could do to resist the gravity that would pull me into the pit that had claimed her. Helplessness, abject ignorance, and worst of all, total failure in communicating with her in any way that made the slightest difference made me someone I could hardly recognize. I seemed to manage almost without notice the other parts of my life, and I went along with surprising evenness—on the surface. I tried to continue to be what I had been for the other girls, and though they missed me and said so, I never felt we lost our closeness or even good times.

Mel and I floundered together through the enigma of Becky's disease, each often distraught by the way the other handled a new crisis for her or confronted her self-destructive behavior. When we tried to escape the overwhelmingness of the disease by just going out for dinner, try as we might, we talked of nothing but Becky. Sometimes we called Dr. Grosser if there happened to be a particularly crucial decision to be made. Our time together, except with friends or family, was bleak and unconnected. We were too often concerned with how to handle the financial and emotional drain that left us depleted, each in our own way. Mel was a natural worrier, and I hesitated to increase his stress by telling of my deepest fears and discouragements. He had enough to manage in keeping us afloat amid the expenses. His worst times were yet to come, when Becky's flushing meals and dollars down the toilet would drive him almost to distraction. I wanted to keep the household as happy as possible and myself in shape to handle the demands of all that kept me alive. Mel was raised in a background of Depression-years pessimism and fear—reality, he would call it. I had grown up during the same years, but I was a product of a family buoyancy that insisted that things indeed did work out. Becky's illness accentuated our differences, even as it drew us into shared concerns. All we could both do was the best we knew how.

But, oh, the mistakes we made. In 1971–73, even with help from a doctor and a psychologist, how did we know anything about bulimia and anorexia? I know now I did everything wrong. A list of the right things to do, from a 1988 *National On-Campus Report* (Magna Publications, Madison, Wisconsin), says:

> *Don't ask her how much she weighs. . . . Stay out of the eating disorder.* Do not *get into a struggle with her over the issue of food. . . . If you try to control her, she will win every time. Be supportive . . . but don't try to be a therapist. Let her handle her responsibilities, even if it seems she's incapable of doing so. Most important,* Make her responsible for the consequences of her behavior. *If after a binging episode, she doesn't clean the bathroom . . . you have the right to say that it bothers you. And if she's taking your food, make it understood that she's got to replace it. . . . If she's frequently moody, tell her that her mood swings are hard for everybody to live with.*

And what I most needed to hear then: "Change will not occur overnight. People do have relapses. If you get too involved, you'll become angry and end up burning yourself out."

I did burn out, probably in ways I never knew. I felt myself fighting despair and helplessness daily as if I were in a cage of wild ferrets going for my throat. I longed to have Becky back, even to be able to imagine her having a life that would replenish and fulfill her.

Out of the hospital

CHAPTER 6

After Hospitalization

Living at Home

Time meant nothing to me. I don't remember holidays like Thanksgiving or Christmas that year, nor even whether or not I was home for them. I just felt numb during those months. Dr. Grosser had a psychologist, Dr. Steven Zlutnick, meet with me and the family. I liked him because he seemed enthusiastic and had a lot of good ideas about constructive ways for me to get along at home and manage my problems. Some of his programs worked, and others didn't. For some reason, he had me weigh in at the hospital every day; that didn't work because I could just eat and throw up and stay the same weight. Although I liked Dr. Zlutnick very much and would have wanted to please him if I had been healthy, I felt incapable of doing anything right, no matter who encouraged me. I don't remember feeling angry, just helpless.

One suggestion of his that did work was a relaxation technique. Over a period of two or three visits, one a week, he taught me to imagine that each part of my body was extremely heavy so that I could sleep better and control my actions. I felt as if he honestly cared about me.

Even when the lithium and imipramine began to work, the changes were gradual. The biggest change was in how I felt about seeing other people.

I remember that for months I felt as though there was nowhere I was comfortable or could ever be comfortable. I felt I didn't belong anywhere. I remember having my parents take me to different places in January and February of 1971 to show me where I could stay instead of at home. I knew I couldn't stand it to stay in one of those places because there were such horrible people there who seemed a lot worse off than I was. I couldn't stand to stay in an institution, especially one like the County Hospital.

I had no feeling for anyone and no idea how it had affected my parents to even think of putting me in such a place. I certainly didn't know that they were consulting with the best experts they could find and were more desperate than I was. I vaguely remember going to the outpatient department of the county hospital. I couldn't drive, so one of my parents took me every morning for a few hours. I hardly remember anything about the craft projects I did, only that I hated being there. The counselor in charge seemed ridiculous to me when she tried to get me involved in something I had absolutely no interest in. Sometimes she even came to visit me at home, and all I wanted was for her to leave me alone.

HER MOTHER'S STORY:
Recovery at Home

Ironically, as Becky gained enough sense of wanting herself back, she began throwing up constantly and taking laxatives by the bottle to try to maintain her unrealistic weight. We knew she shoplifted these whenever she was on her own and that she began dating boys just to get out of the house and be where stores were. We talked with our neighborhood pharmacist about reimbursing him and urged him to let Becky know he was watching her. But then she just went to other places.

Dr. Grosser came out of his office one day to talk to me in the hall after seeing Becky. "She has a disease we're only beginning to find out about," he said. "It's called anorexia nervosa." He explained that it was a compulsion to attain and stay at an unreasonable weight and that it could take over a person so completely it could destroy her. Becky had two aims: to get down to 105 pounds and to get back to Seattle.

I slept outside her room as I had when she was sick as a child, but now it was to make sure she didn't slip off in the night to thumb a ride or otherwise talk a stranger into taking her back to Seattle. Once when she disappeared, the whole family and a couple of boyfriends combed the neighborhood until we found her five blocks from home, actually about to get into a car with a man. Frustrated, she fought our rescue like a frightened deer, wide-eyed and desperate.

That spring of 1971 we were grasping to find somewhere or something that could alter Becky's circumstances enough that she could begin to feel as if she really were getting better. Living around the family seemed like daily defeat to her, as others went about their business with school, jobs, dates, and projects.

At the recommendation of Dr. Grosser and a social worker, Becky moved into a home-living center at the university and registered for school. It seemed like a very risky thing. If it was so hard for her at home and she was so completely unaware of the feelings or activities of others around her, how would it be with a roommate and a dozen other students living near? And would she be able to make it in school?

Dr. Grosser had explained that with mental illness, the first sign of trouble is ignoring personal hygiene. The second is being unable to concentrate enough to do any kind of studying. Becky's sense of herself, except for being conscious of her weight, was still dim, and her attention span was fleeting. We were cautious in hoping for even minimal success. But something had to move her from the dismal futility of the sleeping–eating–throwing up routine that had taken over her life.

Becky wanted to try the new environment, and we let her register, with more hope than we had had for a year. Part of the reason for our liking the home-living center as a sort of halfway place was that it was well supervised and yet full of healthy adults going to college. But we had no idea of what her real life was like. She lasted out the quarter and then moved home, even more unhealthy and unhappy in March than she had been in January.

CHAPTER 7

Two Days in Becky's Life:

1971 and 1989

1971

Age 20. Always alone or trying to be. Staying for one quarter at the Sill Home Living Center on campus, seeing my friends and roommate in only superficial, perfunctory ways. The irony: living in the Center as part of taking a class in Foods and Nutrition. Totally bored with school, this class even more than others.

9 A.M. (about) Awake full of resolution, "I'm not going to do it today." Drag out of bed to get to 9:55 class at the U. Don't care how I look. No breakfast. Easy. Never liked it. Sit in class, English lit., lost, unprepared, in a daze, not knowing what's going on.

10:50 A.M. Run to the candy machine in the hall, get a big chocolate chip cookie. Down it.

11:05 A.M. Another class, philosophy, in the auditorium. Pay no attention. Planning what I'll eat for lunch.

Noon. In the old orange Maverick shared with my younger sister but used mostly by me. To the Hungry Guy, fast-food college hangout. Have a hamburger, fries, a chocolate shake.

To the Red Apple Restaurant downtown. Have soup, salad, pastrami sandwich, drink.

Back to the campus, to the 7-11. Have Twinkies, more ice cream—Haagen-Dazs.

About 1 P.M.   To Smith's Food King or some other super-market with huge bag/purse. Just throw stuff in, whatever looks good—Hostess cupcakes, candy bars, a package of cashews, sometimes cheese, packages of meat, some bread, but mostly sweets, especially containers of ice cream that were so easy to throw up. Must have been pretty good at the shoplifting never to get caught. Back to the Sill Center to pig out, often lying down on my side almost in a fetal position to experience the comfort and security of eating alone. No one could intrude on my little world. Then throw up by putting finger down my throat. Five or six times in the afternoon, while my roommate is in classes or gone with boys. The whole day planned around what to eat next and how to get it, where to go to throw up.

6 P.M.   Dinner at the Center. Really good. Girls put main meals on for each other; our grades depend on appearance of the food as well as taste. Enjoyable conversations, but I don't care. Only about eating fast and a lot—five courses, three rolls, pie or cobbler with ice cream for dessert. Most of all getting away after to get rid of all the food.

7 P.M.   (about) Across the parking lot to the Union Build-ing or to our room alone to throw up. Try to hide it. Try most often to find a public rest room that is totally unoc-cupied. Frantic. On going anywhere, always figure where every bathroom is and whether I'd have to go somewhere else. Often throw up six or more times in a row. Some-times it's hard, takes a while. Have to get going. Then feel totally exhausted and drained. Three or four times a week take laxatives—a whole bottle of Correctol. Shoplifted to get it, never feel guilty. I had to get rid of the food. But no matter what I do, I feel rotten.

All night. Sick as a dog, nauseated, waking up, taking laxatives, thinking, "I can't get fat, no matter what." But also, "Oh, I've got to eat *everything* I want to eat. I hate the way I feel, but as long as I don't gain weight, it's worth it."

I was all by myself. I never really thought about how anyone else saw me. It was such a lonesome problem. I was totally unaware that I was digging a chasm between me and everyone around. I couldn't have cared less about anything or anybody. No one could have told me I was addicted to the whole destructive process.

1989

Age 37. Almost always with others. Married to Paul, a real estate broker and writer. Living with our three sons in a four-bedroom, three-bathroom home, one of the bedrooms turned into a workshop for me to do stained glass. Out of every window a view of the Wasatch Mountains or Salt Lake Valley.

7 A.M. Nick, fifteen, wakes up Richard, thirteen, for school (junior high). They shower, fix cereal and juice for their breakfast. Nick has an external fixation on his left lower leg, pins to set tibia and fibula bones, broken when a car turned into him on his bike three weeks ago.

7:15 A.M. Nick on crutches. Paul drives him to Jazz Band. Returns to meditate, shower, have breakfast.

7:45 A.M. (about) I'm up. Have bran cereal, apple juice, a hot bath. Watch "Good Morning America."

8 A.M. (about) Michael, six, is up, to kisses and hugs. I love it! He has breakfast at the bar while I clean up, visit with him, and straighten the house.

9 A.M. One day a week, tennis with friends. Other days, I attend a real estate class to become a sales agent, something I've thought about doing for a long time. Drop Michael at baby-sitter's with his best friend, Ryan.

12:15 P.M.   Pick Michael up; drive him to kindergarten.

12:30 P.M.   Lunch, if home: most days, one slice of whole wheat bread, a chicken breast or turkey, sliced apple. Sometimes—rare—pastrami or Reuben when eating out. Usually a salad. Once a week or so, I splurge and have that at home. But I'm never tempted to just keep eating like I used to, and the idea of throwing up is totally repulsive to me now. This winter, when I had a stomach flu, I threw up over and over for a night and a morning and couldn't stand the feeling. I wondered how I could possibly have done what I did.

1–2:30 P.M.   Might do some errands—to the post office, the bank, the cleaners, the grocery, etc. Back at home to work in art room on commissioned stained-glass pieces, feed two cats, hold and pet them. Every day at least one load of wash, folding, or working in the yard. I don't love this, but I love being outside. Talk on the phone sometimes to firm up plans for lunch with friends—about twice a week—with sisters and mother on Thursdays.

1 P.M.   (about) Paul sometimes home for quick lunch— turkey sandwich, apple, 2% milk.

2:30 P.M.   (about) If I haven't run at 6:30 A.M. with Paul or some friends, I go for a run at the nearby high school track and feel great after.

Midafternoon.   A Jonathan apple and diet Dr. Pepper or caffeine-free Diet Coke while doing more art work or practicing the piano to accompany church singing on Sunday.

3:40 P.M.   Boys home from school. Typical day: Drive Nick to saxophone lesson or play practice, Richard for campaign treats (for seventh-grade office) or to basketball practice, Michael to gymnastics or just along with me or home with the brother not driven somewhere, playing Beastmaster, slam dunk, or riding his bike, sometimes with a friend who's come over.

4:30 or 5 P.M.   Start fixing dinner, art work in between in spare time. Watch news at 5. Kids play Nintendo or go to friends' houses on bikes. On phone with friends, sisters, or mother while in the kitchen. Drink water or diet pop, always thirsty because of taking lithium.

6 P.M.   Paul home. Dinner, all at the table, talk over the day. Typical meal: spaghetti, green salad, garlic bread, or chicken breast or meat loaf and baked potatoes. Sometimes cream cheese pie or ice cream and cookies for dessert.

Evening   Do stained glass or read or go to a movie with Paul. Boys do homework, watch TV after. Michael plays Nintendo with one of them. Paul often works in real estate. At fifteen, Nick is always starved, has a turkey or pastrami sandwich.

9 P.M.   Make lunches for the boys, trade off with Nick. Turkey or pastrami sandwich, raisins, beef jerky, yogurt, a candy bar.

10 P.M.   Bed. Read to Michael, talk to each about this day, next. Snack before bed: Lemon ice milk; for kids, milk, yogurt, toast; for Paul, Jonathan apples. Read till midnight with Paul.

I feel fulfilled and just plain happy. If I could change anything in my life, it still probably would be my big waist. I would maybe like to lose five pounds—but who wouldn't? Where weight used to rule my life, now what I eat is unimportant compared to what else I enjoy. I never really binge and am not tempted to.

My husband is almost always understanding and patient with me, although he is much less social than I am. He prefers solitude and meditation or being at home with the family to going out. He looks inward for his enjoyment, while I look outward. I adore my children, and they love me. We have always been very close and able to joke around about almost everything. My relationships are good with our two families and with neighbors and people I work with. I feel very, very lucky. And free.

My life in 1989 was typical of how I had lived for fifteen years as a wife and mother who found fulfillment in being at home and using my creativity to do stained glass and raise my family. It was a very unstressful life and I thrived on it.

(Two years later, after the completion of this book, my life is very different. I now have a career in real estate. After six months of struggle to learn the business, I feel successful now. Every day is unpredictable and exciting and sometimes frustrating. I am learning to handle the ups and downs. Sometimes I feel overwhelmed and need time to be alone, but overall, I am glad to be doing what I am. Nick and Richard are now seventeen and fifteen and are more independent. They continue to get good grades and are really good kids and a lot of fun to be with. Michael is eight and a very athletic, sensitive, sweet boy. I only wish I could still give him the time I was able to give before I started working. I'm sure most working mothers have to deal with these trade-offs. Sometimes I feel guilty and even lonesome when he's home after school with his brothers and I'm busy with real estate. But I do feel I have a very rewarding career that makes me more confident as a person even if I'm less available as a mother. I hope that as I get a little more experience, I'll be able to balance these two sides of my life more efficiently.)

CHAPTER 8

The Long Road Back:

1971–73

HER MOTHER'S STORY:

The Struggle

During those three years of recovery, now so long ago, Mel and I struggled in our own ways. Equally concerned, equally anxious to help, equally fumbling in our efforts, we differed primarily in that he could go to work and become involved in a life that shut out any problem at home. Although he suffered the same agonies that I did and we shared the bewilderment night after night, his was most often a life apart.

The closest parallel for me was teaching a 7:45 A.M. class in freshman English three days a week. There I could completely lose myself in a world of ideas and people by doing what I had learned, over twenty-five years, to do and to love. I could go while Becky was still asleep in the morning and be back before she was awake, renewed and ready for another perplexing, demanding day.

No matter how demanding those days were, Paul was always there for us. He was like a son we might have had. Most days he was somewhere in the house, writing poems with Megan, now eight, kidding with one of the other girls, or often in my makeshift study in the storage room talking with me about what he had just read or heard about in a class, planning what we might do to help Becky.

Slowly we acquired more information about Becky's illness. Dr. Grosser told us not to expect Becky's mood swings to be anything like her sisters'—unless she was on medication and it had had time to work. The same kinds of tragedies, mistakes, successes, joys, and woes—that triggered changes in the girls' sense of themselves and the world—had beset all of them. But, Dr. Grosser explained, the other girls likely had had mood swings like this:

while Becky's had been like this:

It was their basic chemical makeup that determined the extent of the swing. Becky's was bipolar, or manic-depressive, the disease so exactly described in that medical dictionary I read after coming home from Seattle. For Becky, it was a chemical imbalance that activated the charge. She would swing from so low as to be suicidal to high enough to have no connection with reality. *Bi*polar meant she was subject to both the highs and the lows, as contrasted with the great majority who suffer only the depression. The state of feeling almost like God is often too euphoric for a person to want to leave it, and so the temptation is there to resist or quit taking medicine like lithium that pulls everything into perspective.

Becky was one of the lucky ones for whom lithium had the right effect: Just take a pill three times a day, have the lithium levels checked once a month for the first year, and be a person free of the destructive impulses brought on at either end of the emotional scale. Becky's condition could be changed, with long months of treatment and love. We resolved over and over to give her the life she had forgotten, the life we so longed for her to have. Dealing with her medicine had to be like setting a broken leg before having physical therapy—the lithium had to take effect before she would be capable of changing any behavior.

102

In the early 1970s, such a biological/chemical approach to treating mental illness was just gaining the credibility it enjoys today. We are thankful that it did, and that lithium and other medicines could give Becky a running start on getting well—if she would let them.

Waiting

It took those three and a half years to get so I cared about anything. I remember being instructed by therapists in the hospital—or later as an outpatient—to make things like tile hot plates or decorative boards. I didn't care about doing a good job or how it looked afterward. Instead of feeling better about myself for having made something, as I used to when I was a little girl, I was just bored. Apathy was all I felt during that time. And hopelessness. I just didn't care about anything.

On one of those boards I made in therapy, I drew a picture of a very thin girl with her hair flying as she surfed in the sun. I pasted a poem by Gwendolyn Brooks next to it:

my dreams, my works, must wait 'til after hell

I hold my honey and I store my bread
In little jars and cabinets of my will.
I label clearly, and each latch and lid
I bid, Be firm 'til I return from hell.

I am very hungry. I am incomplete
And none can tell when I may dine again.
No man can give me any word but Wait,
The puny light. I keep eyes pointed in;
Hoping that, when the devil days of my hurt
Drag out to their last dregs and I resume
On such legs as are left me, in such heart

As I can manage, remember to go home,
My taste will not have turned insensitive
To honey and bread old purity could love.

I didn't even know that I was waiting. I just plodded or slept through my days and felt I had no control over anything.

On the Teeter-Totter

Discouragement is a mild word for what we were feeling during those three years of recovery. So little seemed to make any difference. So often I felt totally fallible and completely frustrated as Becky's recovery bounced from hopeful to hopeless. Two poems catch the extremes of my moods then—the first grim and bleak.

the keys are lost
*(a villanelle to Becky)**

the keys are lost, where can they be found?
in silent places with their jumbled parts
they loosely turn and turn and turn around.

nostalgia twists the need they plumb to sound
tight openings with vacancies for hearts.
the keys are lost and where can they be found?

is it the keys that keep the Keeper bound?
or where they used to fit? what missing starts
the awful turn and turn and turn around?

did thieves thrust early into threads that wound
unwatched and well through years of easy starts?
before the keys were lost, jangling to be found?

*Until Another Day for Butterflies, Salt Lake City, Utah: Parliament Publishers, 1973, p. 141.

*through rings and rings of keys the search is bound
to finger holes that substitute for hearts:
they all will turn and turn and turn around.*

*what combination thrashes for its count?
who knows the will of keys and holes and parts?
the keys are lost and even if they're found
won't they still just turn and turn and turn around?*

The second poem tells of the exuberance I felt when I
sensed a tide turning in Becky, when her real self began
to emerge.

YES!*

*Hey World! Good morning.
Today I'm cured for sure
[and so is she.]
Watch me swing out of bed
and take my tongs to everything
not where it should be!
Dirty clothes,
you're sunk. Weeds, hang on to your roots.
Hunger, you'll be fed—by me, myself.
Personally I'll stir juice and beat with a wooden spoon
and indulge any fancy
that makes it up the stairs.
Take me off. Spirit me away
through petunias and geraniums
and the birch that never really learned
how to cry. I'll catch whatever
you can throw and pin it high
on the grey grapestake that
fences not a thing.*

---

*Until Another Day for Butterflies, Salt Lake City, Utah: Parliament Publishers,
1973, p. 22.

We tried everything we could think of to invite Becky back into life. Neighbors had her over to swim, relatives came to visit, her Aunt Nedra tried to teach her knitting on a machine, knitting that Becky had done so speedily, even left-handed, when she was only nine but that she now tossed aside as she had all of her hobbies. Friends took her for rides. We had blessings given and therapies initiated. We had times that started out full of expectation, when Becky seemed to be getting back to having some interests, but they were short-lived. It was easy to misinterpret how she was and to hope too much that she could get out of herself, even to be entertained.

For instance, Becky had always liked music, so one night her dad and I and her two youngest sisters took her and Paul to see *Fiddler on the Roof* at the university's Kingsbury Hall. As the rest of us got lost in the music and the drama, Becky became more and more restless. She said that she was itching. Was it her medicine? Or boredom? Or both? Before the first act was over, Paul took her home.

Another time, Becky wanted to get a wig. She felt that somehow a new hairstyle could give her a real boost. She and I went shopping and found a not-bad wig that she wore home, smiling with new confidence. It looked so unlike her, though, with its set shape and shine, that no one could be enthusiastic about it, especially Paul. And though no one actually said anything negative, the wig got shunted into the pile of unsuccessful attempts at a comeback via clothes or projects or makeup to cover the complexion ruined by laxatives and purging. Becky's behavior could have been interpreted as very manipulative, but her illness was so severe and consistent that the doctors assured us she had nothing to say about her reactions. I was still convinced that love and improvisation could somehow work to help Becky.

Paul, with Becky wearing her wig

106

One escapade that did work, at least for a week, was a trip that Becky, Megan, and I took to Phoenix, Arizona, between quarters at the university. I had hoped that if Becky could be completely away from any pressure in Salt Lake, we could redirect some of her habits so that the medication could begin to work effectively. I checked the idea out with Mel, Dr. Grosser, and Dr. Zlutnick, and they all thought it was worth a try. The plan was to drive to Phoenix, where Becky had always said she wanted to go, and stay in a motel with a pool—swimming was a favorite activity that she never tired of. We would stay together in quarters close enough so that Becky would have to eat healthy meals and would not be able to escape to throw them up. Taking eight-year-old Megan along was pure serendipity for all of us. Becky loved being with Megan and did not feel threatened by her, and Megan could furnish the diversion that both Becky and I would need during the five days. We saw a movie, shopped, watched some TV, and just spent time together. Knowing that Becky had taken her medicine—I had watched her swallow it—I even took the chance of letting her drive coming home. We took a little-traveled road to visit Bryce Canyon in the snow, and though Becky's driving was a bit scary, all of it was part of some miracle of feeling, for at least that week, that we were back to normal. It all seemed to work, and I came home more hopeful than I had been in maybe two years. Besides, we had had a good time!

BECKY'S STORY:

Tired

Somehow I felt my sisters were doing everything they should and were doing great in the world; yet I had no

Megan, age seven, as she looked
on the trip to Phoenix

ability to feel like one of them, let alone to compete. I felt I was just nothing and always lost and ashamed. Besides, I never really felt healthy during this period. Nothing hurt physically, but I felt like a blob, very slow and heavy, as if I were walking with weights on my extremities.

Mentally and emotionally, I felt that something was very wrong with me. I could not imagine ever seeing an end to my misery. I wanted to get under my covers in bed to hide and escape. Spiritually, I felt deserted. Sometimes I tried to pray late at night when I couldn't sleep, but I never received any reassurance from God, and so I lost my desire to try seeking His help. When our bishop or my uncles gave me a blessing for healing, I was glad at the time and made some resolutions, but they didn't last because I was too sick. I had no control over what was happening to me. Medication was all that seemed to help me, but I hated it and resisted taking it.

As far as my appearance went, what I saw when I looked in the mirror was a plain girl with long brown hair who was too heavy and had tired-looking eyes and very broken-out skin. I felt like a nonentity. I didn't have any idea who I was, so I tried to dress like Rinda because she looked good in her clothes and had a lot of boys asking her out. I even borrowed her clothes without asking her, especially a maroon sweater that was her favorite, and mine, too. But still I hated her for being skinny. Hoping to change my appearance, I became obsessed with the idea of getting a short-haired wig. I was sure it would make me look sophisticated. Like everything else in my life, I tired of this very quickly.

In the months following my hospitalization, mostly I did what my parents planned for me, like going to *Fiddler on the Roof*. I never got excited about going anywhere or doing anything, but since Paul was going, I decided I would. I had started on a different kind of medication, and partway through the play I started to itch all over. Because I couldn't sit another minute, Paul took me home. I was covered with a bad rash.

There were lots of times like this when I was thoroughly embarrassed to be out in public or to be seen anywhere. And yet my parents and the doctors thought it was good for me to get out and experience the real world. The trip that my mother and Megan and I took to Phoenix was wonderfully refreshing to me. I remember feeling a little better; this was a kind of new beginning for me. We all swam and lay in the sun, which began to improve my complexion. I remember letting go and enjoying the world again after years of not being able to. We ate good food in good restaurants (I remember a steak dinner especially). My mother never let me out of her sight, so I knew I couldn't get away with throwing up. I wanted to at first, but then I finally felt that I could eat and not gain weight—without throwing up. When I got home and found I hadn't gained— I was still 110 pounds!—it was the thrill of my life. I even got to drive some coming home. I felt as though something had been lifted from me, and I was in an airplane going through a cloud and coming to the other side, where it was sunnier.

HER MOTHER'S STORY:
Becky and the Family

It was hard to watch Becky on the outskirts of family life. I knew she was comparing herself with her sisters and what must have looked like easy, comfortable lives full of excitement and acceptance of teenage activities. Her exchanges with Shelley, and especially with Rinda, were minimal and usually full of indifference rather than any outward antagonism. They tolerated our meetings with Dr. Grosser and Dr. Zlutnick and might have tried to help, but their relationships with Becky were so uncomfortable that they took the easy route and skirted any clashes by trying not to be part of them. They basically were happy enough themselves when they were with the family, and they felt that the problem was pretty much Becky's. It probably was. I could sense little communication between Becky and the other girls. With her dad, there was none. His was a black-and-white world, born of that kind of upbringing. As kind and gentle as he basically was, Mel's patience with less than acceptable behavior was understandably frayed. And I was as weary as I was desperate. At home, Becky disappeared into some oblivion of her own making, most often into sleep. It seemed apparent that if she were to get well, it would have to be somewhere other than in the shadows of her sisters. But where? To say that life at home was in any way ordinary would be nothing but wishful thinking.

Mel and I had to struggle with our anger as well as concern. Once he and I were called, along with Becky, into the chambers of a judge, when Becky was picked up for taking a blouse from a store. As far as we ever knew, this was the only time she shoplifted anything but laxatives. The judge dismissed her in our custody, and we left very quietly, numbed with disbelief. We knew Becky was not responsible yet for any of her behavior. What we longed for was a chance to make her responsible, but that was still more than a year away.

Mel, humiliated and baffled at the idea of theft in his family, wanted to keep her in her room, as if she were under arrest. I wanted to do something—anything—to jar her into reality. What a nightmare it was to find, among so much else, that your daughter was shoplifting.

On a typical night, Becky and I had one of our usual heart-to-heart talks into the wee hours. As always, I indulged my wishful thinking that morning might bring some new way of going. I remember pretending to myself during the night that I really hadn't heard the sound of the toilet flushing over and over again downstairs. Denial. How else could I even begin to deal with what I knew was actually taking place?

The next morning, as I started making breakfast in the kitchen, I found that all the bread for toast was gone. The cookie jar was empty. All the leftovers in the refrigerator that I had saved for dinner—pot roast, carrots, potatoes, even gravy—had disappeared. I found Becky curled up on her bed with her sleeping bag over her, buried in oblivion. I couldn't stand it. The waste! The incredible flushing down the toilet of herself—and all that food! And the medicine! Any effort, angry or gentle, to rouse Becky out of the repetitive misery that was burying us all was pure futility.

I woke her, told her to dress, and ordered her into the car. We drove to the nearest bakery, both of us sullen and silent. I told her to come in with me and, standing in front of the display cases, had her tell the puzzled saleswoman what she would most like to buy. We left with bags of sweet rolls, cookies, bread, even a cake—with layers of frosting. My boiling point had been reached. In the car I said, "OK, if you want to eat so much, go ahead and eat every crumb. Eat until you're so sick of eating that you really do have to throw up." I had some nutty notion that I could cure her by overdose, or by aversion therapy, something I had heard about for smokers trying to quit. What folly. Stupid, frustrated, irrational folly.

I would have tried anything, but nothing would have worked. All that resulted from any of the angry outbursts or mandates was more despair on my part and more sneakiness on Becky's. At that point, nothing seemed to make a difference. What we really needed most was for her medicine to stay down long enough to take effect.

Anger

At home, whenever no one was in the kitchen, I would go first to the bread drawer and get half a loaf and then to the fridge to see what I could find that was starchy or rich. I would quickly go downstairs before anyone could see me and eat the food while lying in bed. The bread especially was soothing. I would fold a piece in half and then over again and just thoroughly enjoy eating it. Then I would take a long nap and have exotic dreams with beautiful rainbows in them. In my mind, I could escape from my dreary world.

Then I would wake up and realize that I had to get rid of the food I had eaten. I'd rush into the bathroom to throw up. Sometimes my mother or sisters—or, worst of all, my dad—would pound on the locked door, telling me to come out. I was always angry. I would rush past whoever was there and go watch TV. I kept all my anger inside and couldn't communicate how I felt to anyone.

I got mad at everybody who tried to interfere with my habit, but the person I was maddest at was my dad. Not only was being the oldest daughter hard for me, but it seemed that he criticized my every move at meals and anywhere else in the house. With my perspective so skewed, it seemed I had never in my life done anything right in his eyes. His constant disapproval turned me in the other direction, making me defiant against whatever he wanted me to do. It would take years for me to learn to appreciate him as the kind and hard-working man he was, who really loved me and didn't know how to show it.

CHAPTER 9

Fumbling Toward Recovery

A Job, a Place to Stay

A friend of mine in financial aid at the university, Ruth Willes, understood Becky's situation and found her the first of several waitressing jobs she held during the spring of 1971. Becky thought this was what she wanted. Although it was around food, such work required little sitting still or concentration, and Becky could be in an atmosphere that she once enjoyed. Looking back, I guess nothing could have been less likely to last. Becky was simply not ready to exert the effort it took to waitress for even two or three hours a day. Besides, being around food led to disaster and contributed further to her sense of failure.

Following our trip to Phoenix, I talked to some young friends, sisters Sue and Linda Budd, who lived in an apartment near the university, where they were both taking classes. They agreed to invite Becky to stay with them. She would pay her part of the rent and food, but they insisted on nothing more. They welcomed her warmly and tried to include her in chats at the table, reading, TV, anything they were doing. She had known the young women, Sue especially, as friends in the neighborhood who had tended her and her sisters growing up. As much as the Budd sisters basically liked Becky, they recognized, within a few weeks, that it was beyond them to influence or live with Becky's behavior. They asked me to try to find another place for her to live.

While she was with the Budd sisters, Becky enrolled with Paul in a Bible class taught by a legendary teacher who Paul thought would interest them both. However, systematic reading and thinking were not yet possible for Becky. She ended up sleeping through the class the few mornings she attended, and then withdrawing from the class so she could sleep in bed.

BECKY'S STORY:

Trying for a Job, a Place to Get Well

I knew that I was causing trouble no matter where I went. At home, I felt unwanted because of my going there only to eat. I felt totally separated from my sisters. We never talked. Although we met as a family with Dr. Grosser and Dr. Zlutnick, whom I liked very much, I don't remember anything they suggested. I only knew that I was supposed to be on some routine that I mostly ignored.

It was hard to be at home because I felt alienated, and I knew it was my fault. When my mother arranged for various places for me to stay, like with two sisters a little older than I was and later at the sorority house, I didn't care one way or another. I just needed a place to sleep and eat and weigh myself. The people didn't matter at all.

I continued my cycle of bingeing and throwing up while I lived in the apartment with our two friends. I still slept a lot in the daytime. Paul would come during the day and try to get me interested in some scholastic ideas or going out someplace with him. But I could barely keep my eyes open. He wanted me to read some books with him, but I just could not stay awake, no matter how hard I tried. I had always been a good reader in high school, especially in AP [Advanced Placement] English. I enjoyed reading essays and profound thoughts and analyzing them. But now, because of my medication, my eyelids felt as if there was lead on them. I would try to open my eyes, but they would just close immediately. There was no way I could get through even one page of a book. I couldn't understand why Paul enjoyed the Bible class so much. I remember sitting there once. It was totally over my head. I only wanted to sleep and fade away. I couldn't wait to get back to the bed in the apartment, which was a mattress on the floor with huge decorative pillows on it. To me, that bed was so comfortable and warm and heaven to curl up on. On campus, I felt totally out of it, like a non-person walking around. I was taking lithium, which I was still getting used to, but my lack of energy had to be due to my diet too. I didn't realize how much I was hurting my body in all those months and years of abuse.

HER MOTHER'S STORY:

Return to Seattle

None of us could know what those years of abuse were doing to Becky, but it was easily apparent that the destruction was whittling away at her whole system. A year later, in the spring of 1972, I would write in my journal:

At home severe complications for Becky. Kidney damage from years of strain—laxatives, now diuretics—found in waste basket, bottles, bottles. . . . What a way to go. Now protein in the urine—poor tired kidneys. Trying so desperately to slough off the pounds via purgatives and delusions. And poor confused Beck willing to put anything on the altar of the mystic 105 pounds, the key to esteem and promise. Even her life.

Becky's once perfect teeth became gray, and her skin broke out more and more. But for her there seemed to be no correlating of cause and effect; or, if there was, she did not seem to be able to implement, for more than a brief time, any resolution to change.

During the years when the girls were younger, trips had been a big part of our life together. The girls remembered happy weeks at the cabin, at the beach, at Lake Powell with the boat. Why not try now to have some away time with Becky? We had not done this since our fateful trip to Newport the summer when everything was falling apart for her.

By the summer of 1971, we felt it might be time to try this. We were invited to Seattle, to the wedding of Shauna Cooney, the daughter of our friends whose house was by the dock where Becky had water-skied. Shauna's fiancé was the medical student who helped me get Becky to the doctor and then home a year before. Visiting their place again and having fun with the wedding festivities would also give us the chance to take Becky back to where she had been so happy.

What we failed to calculate was the enormity of her despair in visiting the place where manic calamity had catapulted her into the bare life she now had. Being there was a terrible kind of *déjà vu* for me, and I ached as I thought how it must be for Becky. It was a terrible encounter with reality.

BECKY'S STORY:

Seattle Again

I think I looked forward to the trip to Seattle because I had hopes of going back to the campus and seeing some of the people I'd met while I was there a year before. I knew that I wasn't the same person I had been. I knew that I looked very different because I had gained so much weight. I was still very aware of it. I even took the bathroom scale in my suitcase. When we saw our friends, the Cooneys, I felt very uncomfortable because of what they knew about me and had seen when I had my breakdown. At the wedding, I felt ugly and didn't want to be there, but I remember it was a beautiful setting.

When I took my family back to the fraternity house where I had stayed, nothing was the same. It was a very depressing feeling to look at the rooms where we had been. All the people I had known were gone, and the whole campus seemed different—the buildings, the streets, the entire atmosphere was changed from when I was there in my glory. It was such a disappointment, I was sorry I had gone back, but it made me aware that my ideas about Seattle were only fantasies that I could never return to. I had built it up in my mind so much, but now Seattle was only a city, and now the meaning and importance of it were gone.

HER MOTHER'S STORY:

Flaming Gorge

It sounded like more fun than anything during that summer of 1971—a trip in a rented camper with our boat on the back, with old neighborhood friends whose families had vacationed with ours for over a decade—a five-hour drive to Flaming Gorge, a lake backed up by a dam four hundred feet deep, tucked in among pine-covered mountains. There was silky-smooth water to fish and swim in and water-ski on, campgrounds for bonfires, stories, games, singing. And with clean, commodious restrooms! Luxury.

Paul wanted to go also. Being in a camper would make the traveling less tedious than it might be otherwise. Becky could sleep if she wanted to, while the others traded around from car to camper doing whatever they felt like—reading, playing games at the little table, napping. And once there, maybe Becky might even like to ski on that gorgeous lake and swim! She had been a water baby all her life. And, of course, she had loved the sun, lying out on the motor mount on hot July days. We would have good, but not-too-heavy food, and the younger girls could snack with their friends on the candy and cookies they knew they would be bringing. How could anything go wrong?

BECKY'S STORY:

Flaming Gorge

I remember feeling that the family was dragging me to Flaming Gorge. They enjoyed water-skiing, and I had enjoyed it before I was sick, but now it was just an effortful activity that didn't sound like fun to me at all. Riding in the camper was a lot better than riding in a car, and Paul came with us and was great. He was cute and fun and like a member of the family. And yet sometimes I didn't care if he was there or not; I would be very indifferent to him, as I was to everyone else.

I remember going on the boat and just lying in the bow and liking the motion of the water that rocked me to sleep. I felt so weak that I had no desire to water-ski or even swim, which for me was very unusual since I had always loved the water, especially a lake.

One night Paul and the family and the several other families who had gone with us were hunting "snipes," a game that seemed silly to me. I was desperate to throw up the dinner I had eaten, and I walked off in the dark alone. I tripped and hit my front tooth on a rock and chipped it. It seemed to me that everyone in the group knew what had happened, and I felt ridiculous. I was so embarrassed to show anyone that it had chipped that it ruined the whole trip for me. I'd had it with being dragged anywhere. I decided that was the last time I would go on the boat.

No one knew how hard I tried not to throw up. I'd try every day, but it ruled my life. Something had to happen to get me on another track.

Finding a Home Away from Home

For all we could tell, everything was harder for Becky at home. We had to find a place for her where she could feel okay, where she could be supervised in benign and effective ways so that she would take her medicine, eat regularly, and not feel that she had to prove herself to anyone by throwing up to stay thin. But where? No such midway place seemed to exist. So we just kept trying one thing after another. (Little wonder that more than ten years later I would be an ardent supporter of a halfway home instituted and built by a forward-looking county mental health board. In 1972–73, such a thing was unthought of.)

Another mistake we made was to try letting Becky live at the sorority house. By then, it was the spring of 1972, over a year and a half since her first hospitalization. I was down after back surgery, her sisters and dad were managing the home, and Becky wanted very much to be away. It was convenient to rationalize that living in the house might spur Becky on to try to get back to herself among the girls she had liked so much. She was returning to school; perhaps being on campus would help her to renew some of her old interests. And in the sorority house she would have to consider the feelings of others if only for her own sense of self. What nonsense, what misguided desperation—for everyone concerned.

At the Sorority House

When I moved out, I knew that it was because the family wanted me to, although no one came right out and said it. For me, it was just a chance to live away.

At home, my sisters were really nice to me, yet they couldn't understand anything I was doing. They talked to me about diet, like planning spinach and fish dinners, and Shelley, who was an artist, talked to me about her work. I was barely interested; I had no idea what art would give me later on. Food was still my only concern.

But the sorority house was a nightmare. I felt self-conscious around the girls and thought, I'm not the same as I was when they knew me before. I took laxatives almost every night and was bothering them by using the bathroom when they were trying to sleep. When one girl who was training to be a nurse confronted me and told me I was sick, I became angry and defensive and wanted to move out. Even anger felt like a sort of emptiness—like how I felt about my mother on that morning when she dragged me to the bakery. It would scare me if she ever got really mad, maybe because she didn't very often—like one time in front of the sorority house when we had had a big argument about my throwing up there the night before. I didn't care that my roommate had talked to her or that I might have to leave.

Another girl who was my roommate tried everything to help me, such as having me write down a schedule for every day and planning rewards if I didn't do anything negative. She was understanding and sympathetic, yet I was helpless. I didn't resent her, but I was just not ready to help myself. I lost track of her when I moved out of the house, embarrassed and disgraced.

_____

HER MOTHER'S STORY:

One sunny day in May, Becky decided that her best cure would be to go to the cabin, alone. Only fifteen minutes from home, but affording total seclusion, this was the place of joy and sustenance for her, growing up. For all of us, it had always been a safe place. Becky felt that if she could go there in the green woods and mountains, in the comfortable familiarity, she could be completely away from food that would tempt her to binge. She felt that she could find restoration on her own. Knowing no one else would be in the canyon at that time of year, anxious but hopeful, I dropped her off there for supposedly two days and one night. It was a gutsy thing for her to try, and I thought, Good for you, Beck, go for it. I prayed a lot, and I did drive up the next day to see how she was doing. She seemed alive with new vigor. She said she had been walking, reading, sleeping, and eating only the healthy, small amounts of food she had brought with her. I drove home feeling some of what I thought I saw shining in her. Could this possibly be the start of her initiating her own program of recovery? Or was I just so in need of thinking that that I would believe anything?

BECKY'S STORY:

I thought the cabin would be a good retreat for me. I remember feeling that maybe I'd be able to conquer some of my problems on my own. But at the cabin, I felt totally blah, like nothing. Even there, I was obsessed with food. I felt like a bear. I just wanted to hibernate and never come out. I couldn't enjoy anything. Even though it was spring and sunny, I felt that it was all dark. I felt only the eeriness of being alone. I had only a certain amount of food for each day, to get me by for each meal, but I ate one day's worth all at one time and then threw it up. Then I just slept; I loved to go into that world of dreams. When my mother came, I told her I'd been walking and reading and enjoying the beautiful canyon, but actually I was still the same as I had been for months. I felt really weak most of the time and never felt like exercising. When I got home, I was as despondent as I had ever been.

CHAPTER 10

Family Crises

HER MOTHER'S STORY:

Back Surgery

What a mess. In February 1972, I needed back surgery. Twenty-three years and five babies before, I had injured my lower back skiing off a cliff and landing in a pine tree. I had long since learned to live with the pain in my back, but now the pain in my left leg became intolerable. How in the world could I ever manage a spinal fusion? Fortunately, I didn't know when I agreed to the operation that it would mean thirty-one days in the hospital, four months in bed, and a year before I could resume a normal life. I started a journal then. The week before my operation:

2/21/72 4 A.M. . . . Pain [has to be] as precious as joy. Too bad to miss it. Must reduce the blessedness of relief. . . . Pain is not the real worry to me—unless way down, subliminal. (Who knows why I'm awake?) Nothing is hard that has a visible end. The pain of helplessness, ineptitude, uncertainty [with Becky]—no comparison. Maybe the past year and a half has prepared me in strange ways to recognize physical pain for what it is—a palpable, manageable, controllable ally whose presence can function for warning, catharsis and cleansing. Not that I welcome it—far from it—but either calculably or by grace of Time, I'll be well to be what I need and want to be. No wonder the ascetics felt purged. I wonder how tomorrow will play on my lowest strings. Oh, Becky, when will you stop hurting?

In the meantime, Becky had wanted to get back into school, but instead of registering for less demanding classes like physical education or typing, she chose to be back in English, much against the advice of Dr. Grosser. He said that the ability to concentrate was one of the first things to go and the last to come back—like grooming on a physical level. He was right. Nothing was easy.

BECKY'S STORY:
Back in Class

My mother was flat in bed after her back surgery, and I was too busy thinking about my weight and my own problems to care about her. I must have been in a state of oblivion.

I had fallen behind in school because I couldn't function, let alone study, so I took most of my classes pass/fail and managed to get by somehow. I remember one class in English literature that I would go to each day, and the professor would assign things to read, way too many pages, it seemed to me. I would go the next day and take a test and get a D. In the mental state I was in, it was impossible to do the work. A friend next to me would get A's on every test; she seemed so intelligent to me. I couldn't conceive how anybody could keep up with that amount of reading. I would compare myself with her and feel like a total failure. I remember taking a folklore class and having my mother help me with a term paper for it, but I don't even

126

remember that she was in bed. I didn't care about anything that went on around me.

HER MOTHER'S STORY:

Being (a) Patient

While I was in pain, I began to have new understanding for what Becky had been going through, even her distance and lack of interest. I found myself as oblivious as Becky had been to all but myself.

---

*Triumph**

Nothing is more self-possessed than pain.
More certain of a place.
More aware of making everything aware.
It's dogged in its occupation,
Thorough in its coup.
Ambition, interest, civility and pride,
desire, curiosity,
hope,
and finally love
Give silent, sullen ground.
And pain parades
in a hollow hall.

By the time I came home on March 26, the "hollow hall" had become my more usual self, at least alive to the people around me. Accommodation to the activity of regular living, however, was hard. I yearned simply to be able to get up and do even the simplest jobs, if only to balance the constant stress of still trying to be mediator and arranger for Becky from my bed. The house teemed with the activities of the others, who were now between eleven

---

**Until Another Day for Butterflies,* Salt Lake City, Utah: Parliament Publishers, 1973, p. 18.

and eighteen and remarkably willing and able to take over keeping the house. Becky was living in the sorority house, but not for long.

Fri. April 14, 47th day . . . My room open to all anytime. Bombardment of everything screened in hospital [visitors, girls' doings—like campaigns for elections at school, dates, plans for trips, even picnics on the bed. So ordinarily fun to be] in the middle. . . . Then [my friend] Virginia, kind emissary of house girls, telling me Becky's throwing up twice every day. Oh! Oh! Dr. Grosser. Calls. Becky back for weekend. Eats. Eats. Food is all.

BECKY'S STORY:
Oblivious to Life at Home

Whenever I was at home, I wanted everyone to leave me alone so that I could sleep or eat. The only time I felt interested or excited about anything was when a boy came to pick me up to go somewhere. It had to be other boys that I didn't know as well as Paul. At this point, I felt that he was more like a brother to me. Yet I enjoyed knowing he was somewhere around the house because it made me feel secure and that someone cared what I was doing.

One night I was in my room, and my father said some boys were there to see me. It took me about twenty minutes to choose something to wear, and even then I remember feeling ugly and fat. I was heavier than I wanted to be at 123 pounds and was very self-conscious about my weight. I had no idea why I gained, even with taking laxatives and throwing up. Now I know that my system was so mixed up from never digesting food in an ordinary way that my metabolism was all off. I couldn't eat anything and let it digest properly.

Probably one of the boys wanted to ask me out, but when I finally entered the living room that night, the three of them were not happy about having had to wait so long.

We talked for a few minutes, and then they left. I felt numb and told myself I didn't really care. In the back of my mind I knew my mother was down in bed, but now I was unable to talk about my feelings to anyone, even her. I was ashamed of everything I was doing and didn't want her to find out. Sometimes she called me into her room and we talked, but it didn't make any difference.

I didn't really want to change. It wasn't till I got a job I cared about that I was able to concentrate on something besides myself.

HER MOTHER'S STORY:

Managing from Bed

As I willed myself to get well, I wrote:

Sun. A.M. April 16, 1972. Less pain, but all the time still. So tired so quickly when up . . . Becky sleeping downstairs. . . . Last night when she came home from the sorority house, her presence like a treatise on tension. How one person can react, spread feeling, turn a household till now easy with my being down, into layers of discontent. Even I can't believe the spreading from mostly her stalking the kitchen and then slipping off to a bathroom to get rid of any scrap or feast she's taken in. Everyone aware of it. No one able to confront it. Everyone tired too. Mel adrift in worry, spent, needing to have some return to normal, abjectly angry at the waste of food and no doubt weary of having me out of commission, though he's been remarkably accepting of my incapacities. It's to referee the times between him and Becky that I need most to be up. Another blow-up over the lost food. He can't be passive as Dr. Zlutnick recommends. And they can't be together. Why can't we just recognize this and go from there? I want to run. I go cold, brittle inside. Helpless. How can it ever change?

Same Sunday, 4 P.M. Becky is gone—back to the sorority house—low, despondent, needing something no one

seems to be able to give. Oh, Beck. Oh, Beck. So sad, So
lost. Oh, Beck, how? How to try to scramble back into
acceptance when you don't even want to wake up. We talk,
you and I, in deep chasms of repetition and futility. . . .
Let this week somehow work for you.

Becky was soon back home again, having been asked to leave the sorority house. It was urgently apparent that she had to have something—a job, a relationship, an interest—anything that would force her to get out of herself. But what? Finally, we decided that she needed to have responsibility for something she really cared about. How about a car? Since winter, Dr. Grosser had let her drive, but sharing the Maverick with two sisters, all of them buying their own gas, was hardly conducive to a sense of independence. Suppose we could help her with a down payment on a used Pinto and then turn the payments over to her? There was nothing she would rather have. In late spring of 1972, that was the next step.

BECKY'S STORY:

Switchboard

My whole problem was that I didn't *want* to change. During this period, I must have been keeping more food and antidepressants down because I finally began to respond to the medication. I heard about a job opening at the university, on the switchboard. I applied and got the job. This was a major turning point. It was the first time I had been motivated to do something on my own.

The job involved connecting people to various extensions around the campus, working with numbers, and being cheerful. There were fun people that I visited with and got to know, and I was making money and beginning to feel like a person again. My parents arranged for me to buy a green Pinto and to make payments to them on the car to teach me some responsibility. And it worked! Even though I lived at home, I felt independent because of the car. Suddenly, I had something to keep me going and somewhere to be. I feel that the imipramine, together with the lithium, was a kind of jump-start for me that I couldn't have succeeded without.

I had quit school, because in my mental state there was no way I could do both, and the job seemed much more important. For the first time since my illness, I kept a job for more than a week. (In fact, I worked for two years, when I quit to have my first baby.)

Because of the job and the antidepressants, food became a lot less important, and my throwing up decreased. I still did it—actually, I have no idea how often—but I do know that I cut way back on the laxatives, too, because I had to function at work. I took my medication faithfully. One of the women in charge told me I shouldn't be "on drugs." Nobody knew anything about how much these drugs were helping me to get better. I wonder how I could have functioned without them. Or how I could now. A friend of mine with manic-depression got talked out of using lithium. Some of her friends convinced her that she could get along believing in mind over matter, and she ended up back in the psychiatric ward. If I learned anything along the way, it was how much the medication had to do with my getting better and staying better.

As far as my health was concerned, I tried to ignore the way I felt. I always felt lifeless and sick to my stomach and constantly tired. I denied to myself any connection between my inertia and what I continued to do to my body through my addiction to my disease.

HER MOTHER'S STORY:

Becky's Job

Becky's getting back into school, her finding a job that might be satisfying, even her wanting to spend some time with her friends seemed minor compared to her taking even rudimentary care of her body. Any signs of independence brought sparks of hope. But the gray look of purging continued, and her face, already broken out, still plagued her vision of herself. Her once beautiful teeth needed more and more dental attention. She never had a period, and her kidneys had one infection after another. How would she ever be able to have a baby or the family life that she had always talked about wanting? Would it ever end?

From my journal:

Hurting can become so habitual that it's like hair or skin— simply there. I can't remember right now not hurting. And so it gets ignored at surface levels—swathed in conversations, other thinking—till time to sleep. . . . How must it be for her?

Just ready to go to sleep when Becky called to me, desperate, couldn't sleep—thinking of Jay and Seattle. I tried to talk her out of calling him. Old panic back. Knew she'd taken laxatives and was up for the night. . . . No way to sleep. . . . How will she ever find a place—a reason—a person? Oh, Hon, where are the keys? What can I even daydream for you? I have burny eyes. Flat. Thank You God for centers inside me! Oh!

For all of our concerns and efforts to stay in touch with what was happening to Becky, we could never have had any idea what was really happening. The manic side of her disease seemed to be better, but the bulimia still controlled much of her life. We did know, though, that almost imperceptibly, and certainly in a jagged course upward, she seemed to be getting better—at least about taking responsibility and being on her own. And, of course, we were rooting for Paul.

Dating

During the spring and summer of 1972, I was dating a lot. Older boys I didn't even know began to call out of the clear blue, or I would go on line-ups [blind dates]. I still wasn't really feeling attractive, so I wasn't attracted to any of them, even though I kissed some of them. I didn't really enjoy it the way I had when I felt gorgeous, as I used to. I was back to thinking that if I weighed 105 pounds I'd be beautiful and look the way I wanted to.

I got a Twister Board and exercised in front of the TV, and I rode my bike to work in the summer. Both Dr. Grosser and Dr. Zlutnick thought I looked fine and were urging me to be realistic about my weight. I weighed about 117, which, for my five-foot-four build, was anything but heavy, but I never didn't want to lose. I cut way down on what I was eating, again thanks to the antidepressants, and I began to get some joy out of life. I liked dating, having dinner, and going to movies, or just sitting around talking.

Mother's Death

One of the few and mostly good things about my time in bed and being incapacitated was having my own mother around to give me the tender care that only a mother can offer a child. She was a born nurse and loved nothing better than to have someone to fuss over. But she didn't run the household—the girls did. And, as might be expected, having three generations in on any enterprise was not always smooth or without friction. Still, except for Becky's continued unhappiness, we all seemed to accommodate ourselves with relative equanimity to having life at home changed by my limitations.

Still, it was months before I wrote with delight on November 18 and 19, 1972:

Sat. Nov. 18—1 P.M. Hey, hey! Better than in over a year?
13 hrs. sleep—so, so, so mellow. Don't hurt! I don't hurt!
Oh, please let it last. I can manage anything when I feel
like this. Even Megan's German measles, Becky's laxa-
tives. . . . Rinda's strain with [boyfriend], Mother's wor-
rying, Mel's loneliness in Hawaii alone [at a real estate
convention]. Imagine feeling this good! Oh stay, stay!
    Sun. Nov. 19—Mother took us all & Paul to Hotel
Utah for dinner. [Mel still in Hawaii] . . .

The next day, just before Thanksgiving, Mother had the massive heart attack that would kill her in less than six weeks.

Wed. Nov 22—12:30 A.M. Oh, Mother, Mother. It's
Thanksgiving Eve. The table is set . . . the old Tom's
stuffed and in at 200 degrees. . . . The girls all pitched in,
Paul too. . . . Now it's quiet and I'm in the black rocker,
and lonesome. Up there in that bleak hospital room you're
sleeping tonight. . . . Weary beyond caring, are you pulled
there and here both? Where are you looking?

Even as my back got better, Mother's condition got worse. As her heart could pump less and less, she would essentially drown in fluid. We brought her home to her own soft bed for what we knew would be her last days or weeks.

At home, she still had to have oxygen and a catheter. I was grateful to be up and about and able to take care of

Mel, Rinda, Shelley, and
Dinny at Lake Powell,
summer of 1972

her. But I was usually too tired to write in my journal. When Mother was sound asleep, I'd drop into bed. My talks with Becky usually took place very late. She almost always wanted to talk only about Paul. She still seemed unable to be part of what was going on around her.

And just as Becky needed me, it was so hard to let my mother go in those last weeks. Besides, Christmas was her time, and my time for great nostalgia and wishing.

Mon. Dec. 4—1 A.M. Every day one more gamut to run. . . . She's here [Mother] amidst her gentle clutter. . . . Mother, how will I be strong enough not to let you know . . . how much I want to have it different? And Christmas—how? How ever again? . . . Somehow I always expected Mother to outlive me by 20 years.

Wed. Dec. 13—5 P.M. We've had her home for a week—and she's better! She loves being among her own. . . . Boys [my 3 brothers] take turns sleeping on cot by her. I take care of her mornings and the girls, daughters and sisters-in-law, trade off most afternoons. She's bright and fun—and very tired. Everything so tenuous—so limbo. So sad—and yet often I feel she'll be well. Especially when I'm with her— which is 90% of the time . . . Yesterday Rind, Meg and I shopped for her clothesline [outfits for each child and grandchild]. . . . Christmas is coming for her.

Sat. Dec. 16—8 A.M. A terrible precariousness . . . Nothing in me, though, is geared to give up. Christmas seems impossible. . . . Haven't bought a gift on my list. . . . So much in me is her. So different. So alike. And Becky flushes herself down the toilet—back, back. So tired. Thought Becky might respond as she did at first—with her lost tears and concern—but that has given way to distance and despair . . .

12/20—midnight Tonight I gave her a shot of Demerol when we couldn't find [doctor brother] Homer. What a feeling—to relieve someone, especially someone you love, of pain and panic. . . . She continues to amaze us with her calm and humor . . . so weary but always willing to try, still thinking about Christmas—wants so to make it.

Mut's Death

During the whole time I was sick, all I remember of Mut was her just nagging and nagging at me about taking care of myself and not wearing such short skirts and being careful around boys. She never showed any affection to any of the boys I dated but Paul. Somehow she had a natural liking for him. One time she sent us to her cabin for dinner for my birthday. She fixed all my favorite foods and had a lot of special touches, like two napkin rings she had made out of birch bark from the canyon with our names written on each. (Eighteen years later, we still have them.)

During my growing up, Mut would take us to the Hotel Utah Coffee Shop for birthdays. It was my favorite place from the time I was a little girl. It was elegant, and I felt grown up when I got to go there with her. It had a huge aquarium with unusual fish that I loved to gaze at while we waited for our food to come. Mut was a gifted artist and had a way of making things nice or fancy or special. I used to go into her room sometimes and watch while she painted hollyhocks. Wearing her smock, with her palette in her hand, she would paint for hours. I loved the smell of the oils and getting to visit with her. I also remember the opera she played, especially on Saturday. But when I was a teenager, I didn't want to be around her because I knew she would just nag at me.

When she had her heart attack, I was so depressed myself that it didn't affect me much. I remember going to the hospital with my cousins on the night she was in a coma and was expected to die. I did not feel much except very alienated from everyone. I felt unworthy of having her even know I cared.

My Mother's Death

Death, no matter how expected, takes us by surprise. Nothing can really prepare us for the vacancy in our psyches and spaces, especially with a parent. When Mother died, I know that Becky was somewhere in the house, probably with Paul. I remember her crying, and it made me vaguely both happy and sad that she could feel like crying. I remember the sadness in all of us gathered there as we had been every night since Mother had come home, all of my brothers and their wives, Mel and our girls. But I don't remember much else about that last night except that Mother was carried out of her room forever.

12/23/72—midnight. Mother is gone. A few gasps. No real struggle. The vigil is over—and so is my childhood. We clung—we all clung . . . I had my chance to take care of her—to read to her, to bathe her soft little body, to feed her, to give her her last shot, to offer her 7-Up in a little purple goblet. She died as I showed her some baby roses—in a room filled with the tiny flowers she loved and sent. And now she's with strangers [morticians] to her—so alone, so unused to strangers—but Father has her for Christmas. Oh, my dear—how I love you. It's Christmas Eve—your time, for sure. Hold my hand and help me.

Mut's Death

Mut's funeral was a very warm, interesting tribute to her life that I remember only vaguely. I was glad that she thought so highly of Paul that my mother requested that he be a pallbearer. It felt good to me to have him around, and talking to him after about Mut, I felt sorry for talking rudely to her at times when she was alive. Paul had teasingly chided me for the way I treated her. Even though I began to miss her when she was gone, I was still unable to feel anything very deeply.

HER MOTHER'S STORY:
My Mother's Death

Emily Dickinson says, "After great pain, a formal feeling comes . . . like quartz." Returning to life, I felt numb, as Becky must have in her trying to recover. And even more unable to cope than I had felt for the two and a half years since Becky's first bout with depression in the spring of 1970.

Wed. Dec. 27th, 1972, 3 A.M. Our 23rd anniversary. The funeral yesterday was poignant but uplifting. Homer, my oldest brother, put Mother's rings on me. Worst, hardest part. She was so married. . . . Mother is gone and the gap is huge. . . . Even believing as keenly as I do that she is with Father, I still feel far away, terribly alone and lost. I always loved her most when we were apart . . . like when Mel and I were first married and living in Palo Alto. . . .

I found myself assessing and trying to make sense of everything.

Mel is such a kind, gentle, loving boy who has never done anything but good for me. . . . Tried to play tennis—blah—show [we saw] later worse. Then home to Becky in tears—Paul doesn't want to get married. What will she do? 2½ years of depending on Paul? . . . Rinda and [boyfriend] in crisis . . . heavy, heavy. . . . Questions, questions. And me far less sure of much except change. What a year! . . . I've learned and learned—only to know how much I need to learn. Most I know: to love is to be sorely

tried—and greatly blessed. Help me to love enough . . .
Feel as if I have 6 parts out of 10 missing. . . .

How long would it be before the great hovering clouds would blow away?

CHAPTER 11

Becky and Paul:
1973

BECKY'S STORY:

Still Around

In the early spring of 1973, I was taking my medication, and I had a job and a car. I felt better, but I was still throwing up almost every day. Paul was still around. When I was out with another boy, he would come to the house and visit with everyone. They all loved him, and he loved them. He and Megan would build tents under the ping-pong table and spy on me from there when I was in the playroom watching TV with another date. Later, we would laugh about it. Or he would sit in the kitchen and talk for hours with my other sisters and my mother. He seemed to enjoy just hanging around at our house. Once he wrote a poem about my dad and said if he were my dad, he'd be lying on the floor giggling at how lucky he was to have this household of girls.

Paul and I were on and off in our feelings toward each other. Right before a family trip to Hawaii in February, I decided to break up with him just to see what it would be like. All I did on the trip was think about him. There was a guitar player at one of the restaurants who reminded me of Paul. I couldn't wait to get home and see Paul.

In Hawaii

While I was laid up from the back surgery, and then in the following months, I had watched sadly as Becky seemed to use Paul to suit her dating situations. Other boys came and went, as she tried to accommodate to the whims of their asking her out. Boys had always been Becky's connection to worthiness—their opinions, their gracing her with their attentions. As she ricocheted from one to another and from improvement to disaster in her healing, her whole life reflected how she felt they viewed her. Everything else seemed incidental—friends, family, entertainment, school, even a trip to Hawaii. We had planned from the time we knew that back surgery was inevitable, that when I was able to—a year later!—we would take the trip to Hawaii. We had saved for that dream trip ever since the girls were little, planning to go when our youngest, Megan, would be old enough to take in its beauties. Little did we know that it would also be a time when we would all need to get away—a need to recuperate from a year of my incapacity; Becky's illness; how many boyfriend crises for Shelley, Rinda, and Dinny; and Mother's death. And then, in February 1973, came the appointment of Mel as bishop (lay ecclesiastical leader) to 350 single university students meeting as a Mormon congregation. This, in the same year Mel was president-elect of the Utah real estate board. In some ways, Paul's presence had been the one constant in our household. That and faith that everything had to get better.

Hardest for me, and what I wanted most to escape, was playing policeman, judge, and executioner to Becky in a regimen of crime and punishment imposed in 1972 by Dr. Zlutnick in his behavior modification programs. Never was my journal clear of entries like, *"What a way to live! Already she is 'grounded' for going in the kitchen. So nightmarish. Every night I wake up about 4 A.M. and go around and around. Meanwhile, all the others go happily along, cooperative, funny, congenial, loving the world. And all I can ask is Why! Why!"*

But I was such a slow learner. My every instinct was toward peaceful coexistence, loving promotion of whatever needed help. But I needed to learn new ways. *"Sometimes the very best thing I can do for Becky is get really mad, not support what she's doing. Then she really comes through. But I never remember. I always want to be on her side."*

I remembered what Dr. Zlutnick had said, but even a year later: *"We are on another course of trying to change. . . . Crisis—a terrible night with Becky up dozens of times—the old way. Finally with Mel's agony—headache, no sleep. I hate it! Finally told Becky we couldn't live like this, that she'd have to decide for herself how she wants to be and then go on her own. This is ridiculous—years of trying everything there is."*

In Hawaii we all let down, lay in the sun, ate up the luscious scenery and food. But I was never unaware of Becky's defiance and her walking away from anything suggesting closeness. She strode with her left little finger arched stiff and her sunburned face unlighted by even the pools and ocean that she swam in. I was also sick that she had broken up with Paul before we left.

Return to Paul

On the trip to Hawaii, I gained a lot of weight. Because I was around people all the time for three weeks, I had had to give up laxatives. I still ate everything in sight, and so did the rest of the family. Although it was gorgeous over there, because I wasn't close to my sisters, I felt lonely. If I had been thin and beautiful, like when I lost all the weight in college, it would have been great to be in Hawaii, but I remember lying on the beach between Rinda and Dinny and feeling extremely self-conscious about how I looked in my bikini.

I was still so involved in myself that I couldn't really appreciate anything, not even what a privilege it was to get to go to Hawaii. One time I got angry at something like my dad's refusing to let us order soft drinks with lunch, and I started walking away from the hotel. I didn't care where I ended up. I began wondering what it would be like to live in Hawaii and to start a new life there. I was still very alone, wanting something different in my life but not knowing how to make any changes. Just like a little kid who pretends to run away, I thought everyone would be really worried about me, but when no one came to find me, I turned around and waited just outside the hotel. I felt relieved, because I knew that realistically I was not ready to live anywhere on my own.

But it was Paul's not being there that made me long to be home. I realized how much he meant to me and that I didn't care about anyone else. Then I got really scared. What if he had given up on me? I called Paul as soon as I got back and told him for the first time that I loved him. We dated seriously after that, but I continued to date others. I guess I was still too insecure to feel confident enough about anything in the future to tie myself down. In fact, when we became engaged a few days after I got back from Hawaii in February 1972, and Paul gave me a large solitaire diamond, everyone said, "Who are you engaged to?" I had to go and tell two guys I was dating that that was it.

Paul was hesitant at first to push our relationship, but we both knew when we got engaged that it was right. It had a great effect on me. I knew that he loved me no matter what I was like, and that was all that mattered to me. I didn't have to try to be someone else or to impress him. I had always felt that way, but it took being without him for three weeks to make me appreciate what I had. I was ecstatic. Our physical attraction to each other became a big part of our caring. That had never been true for me with anyone else.

We got engaged in February and planned to be married in August. I felt very happy and sure about everything. I wanted to be married. I even had a place to live with my best friend Debbie. Her husband was away in the army reserve, so she invited me to find an apartment with her. I was taking my lithium and imipramine, and Dr. Grosser said my basic chemistry was probably balanced out. The summer before, Dr. Zlutnick had left for another job somewhere else, so I had been responsible just to my parents for about nine months. My life was 90 percent better except for my throwing up—I can't even remember how often, but nothing like a year before.

My father did one thing that really made me determined to succeed: He told the doctors that he thought I couldn't get married, that I couldn't do it. He said, "How can she be able to take care of someone else when she's so helpless herself?" This made me want to show him I could do it all.

HER MOTHER'S STORY:

Paul's Gentleness

When we came home from Hawaii and Becky and Paul became engaged, I hardly dared hope for what seemed at last possible—a life for Becky, and with Paul, whose depth and goodwill I trusted so completely. Maybe one of the elements in that trust was how he treated Adriane, his sister, who had mental retardation. He sometimes took her on dates, to a movie, or for a ride, Becky going along as natural as he was. His whole family made Adriane part of any outing or visit. I respected their honesty and forthrightness and especially their constant kindness. They accepted Becky as her very best self. Their love for her was palpable.

This was, in no way, an ordinary response in the early 1970s, when so little was said about mental illness. What a morass of nonunderstanding we had to come out of. I had grown up in a neighborhood where a girl with mental retardation was hidden away by her family. She was joked about by the kids playing in the street if she made an ungainly, sometimes naked, appearance on her lawn or front porch. She would quickly be snatched back into the darkness of the shame that made us all alert to the inequities of birth and ashamed of ourselves for having been uninvited witnesses to a blight none of us could do anything about but fear or scorn. Somehow Paul's gentleness with Adriane assured me of more than his still young understanding of Becky's illness and his willingness, even eagerness, to make her part of his life.

I just plain loved him, and I hoped, although not without some misgivings, as I hadn't in nearly three years, for the lifting of the shroud that we all had lived under for so long.

Becky and Paul radiant, changed. How long will it last? Paul "outrageously happy" . . . As he says—"it's a religion." Becky & Paul continue to dominate my hopes with a week of happiness. Still can't believe it. So skeptical—so taught to be. This year things so much better. I dare look ahead a day, in fact, a year, ten years. . . . Becky today . . . full of talk about a house with Paul. She seems happy! And with that, so much falls into place. . . . Oh, please let it be real! . . . Picked a huge sunflower on my clear-around-the-block walk today with Beck. Sort of that kind of day. Hooray!

Hawaii had seemed to me a turning point, even though the trip itself had been so half-rewarding.

BECKY'S STORY:

The Ring

I remember March 1, the day I got the ring. Paul had gone to a jewelry store and had it made up especially for me. He spent his life savings on a large diamond solitaire, and I was so honored to think that he was willing to give that up for me that I appreciated him more than I ever had. Somehow this material gift allowed me to begin to love him in a way that deepened with time. Little did I know then that he would have a way of feeding all my needs: spiritually, mentally, physically, and somewhat socially. At first, he even did that, but later on his inward nature began to turn him toward meditation and solitude.

But that spring we still had our ups and downs. We had to learn to get along with each other. He would do certain things that bothered me, like the way he drove his Volkswagen slowly and absentmindedly. Or the way he always hung around the house talking to the family even if I wasn't there. Sometimes I'd come home and he would be there, and if I wasn't in the mood to see him or be with him, I would think of an excuse just to leave. But most of the time, I enjoyed being with him, especially when we were alone and we would go to concerts or to dinner. Our physical relationship was very important at this time, and we were so attracted to each other that we had to hold back. We both wanted to wait till we were married to be really intimate. We set the wedding date for August 25, which seemed about right to me.

In the meantime, I was working at the switchboard and enjoying that and feeling more confident about my looks and weight. But I was still secretly bingeing and throwing up at least once a day. I realized that I was hard to live with because of my throwing up, and I didn't know how I would continue to do it after I was married. Every day I would think, okay, today I'll quit, but I just couldn't do it. I never talked to Paul about it, and he didn't really know it was as big a problem as it was.

Our relationship was essentially simple. I don't remember talking about the future except to decide things about our wedding. We never talked about religion, how many children we would have, who would manage the money, where we would live, whether I would work or not after children, how we felt about family life, nothing about any social aspects of our life together. That somehow things worked out was pure luck. Most important of all, we never talked about my illness. Paul approached it as if I were fine and normal, and he expected me to be that way.

The Still Jagged Course

That spring was a time of turmoil, even with the joy that hovered so tenuously on the horizon. I wanted so much to hope and to assure Becky of my confidence, but experience had acquainted me with a taut wariness that still was foreign to everything in me.

Saturday, May 5, 10 A.M. En route to real estate convention in Las Vegas with Mel . . . so much she [Becky] is willing to sacrifice on that altar of 105 pounds. Even now, the new life of dotted swiss wedding dress, singular diamond, apartment hunting, status in a world she thought she could never occupy. Even the life with Paul, whose love transcends any reason except wanting her.

Later, the night of that same day on the trip with Mel, both of us supposedly away from concern about anything, the old welling of concern for how to help returned. Like Mel, I was always going back to prayer and wishing for omniscience, if not omnipotence.

Beyond any recourse but prayer, the kind she and I can cry together in closeness, knowing so much more than we say. And now only the waiting, the fear, the hope, the faith in the miracle, the not daring to look even to Aug. 25th or a real beginning. In her need, she needs not to need me—and therein lies all the ambivalence for both of us. How I'd love to go back home to bathe her, powder her, put on little white shoes and take her hand for a walk in Liberty Park or the zoo. What didn't I do? What can I do? And the others ease through their days, tossing off crises with concern but aplomb of knowing and being somehow sure. How come? More than perversity of fate; more than system, positioning, conditioning. What? And how to give them joy in themselves through retention of wanting the same for others? No fulfillment is possible without both.

Through late spring, Becky fluctuated between almost-wellness and reverting to old ways. No matter where I was, her situation dominated every view.

May 14, 11 A.M. Lake Powell. Bright. Bright. Red sand, silk lake, pillows in the sky. Tent barely flapping, water's only ripples from far off boats. . . . The quiet finally pervades it all. The healing, the cleansing, the ultimate purging of quiet—natural selection. . . . Everyone aboard the boat except Becky and Paul. How are they doing? Becky adrift in her insecurities, Paul banging against impossibles. Can they moor each other—or only go under with trying? If either had an anchor, or even a rope to throw the other. But our day—Indian ruins, hike, lunch on the boat, sun—blanketed lightly the misgivings, all flowing in the wake of going home.

Summer came, and with it the business of getting into a nonroutine. After Lake Powell and the quiet, no time. Too many people, places, urgencies. And concern about Becky:

June 4, 6:30 A.M. . . . Becky seems bad, nervous. Moved into an ap't alone. This week with Debbie, but everything "my," "mine," "I chose." Where is Paul? Why the whole thing? Mystery. How much do you help? Give things?

She's so unable to get out of herself for a minute. Will this marriage really come off? How can it? And if it does???
. . . I watch and wonder, guarded in my gladness, seeing Becky with a can of diet pop walking sternly into marriage—and disaster? Only now and then the quick radiance, the effervescence that used to be. I can't get thoroughly into anything, for wishing it different.

I didn't know enough yet to recognize all the little differences in how she was getting better. Coming home, I just couldn't get into planning the wedding. Like the sense of storm when the sky is barely clouded, I had so much uncertainty about the future that I subconsciously put off making any reservations, even as I hoped with everything in me that it would all come off. Whether Becky really wanted a big wedding, I could never be sure. I wanted to make it whatever felt right to her, but at that time, not much felt comfortable at all.

BECKY'S STORY:

Paul

When I got back from Hawaii and my feelings changed so much, I remember hoping that Paul would propose. After getting the ring in March, I was much more certain of everything and was sure that I wanted to marry him. I must have been truly in love with him. I did think more than ever, Okay, I've got to stop throwing up. And it became much less important to me because I had other things going on in my life. My self-image was a lot better since I was engaged, and I felt important to him and to other people. The compulsion began to fade away. But even with the imipramine and lithium, and wanting so much not to have Paul find out, I couldn't entirely stop. I still had never really admitted to myself that I was sick, that I had an addiction.

I kind of had a funny feeling about not being up to a

big wedding, so I halfheartedly made plans with my mother, hoping that she would just take over on everything. We bought a wedding dress, which I was very excited about, and bought fabric for bridesmaids' dresses. But Paul and I seemed to be in some kind of limbo, and so was my mother.

I moved into my own apartment and then stayed with Debbie for two weeks. Deb advised me about marriage. She had been married about nine months but seemed like an expert. She and Paul were old junior high school friends, and she liked him a lot. She said that you have to give in sometimes to make things work, so it helped me appreciate Paul and want more than ever to make things work out.

I gave up bingeing and just threw up after regular meals, I think maybe once a day at the most. I remember having a hard time adjusting to having food in my stomach. My way of thinking for years had been that I would gain weight if anything stayed in my system. With other addictions it's possible to break away "cold turkey" and just give up whatever feeds the disease. But with my addiction, food and keeping it down has to be part of the cure. I thought nobody knew that I was still throwing up that spring we were engaged. Paul told me later that he did know.

Therefore, when he told me he couldn't marry me, I was devastated. We were sitting on the couch in the playroom at home talking, and he said, "Becky, everything's off. I can't go through with it." He just left, and I was in a state of denial for a few hours. I went out shopping and ran into my Aunt Kay. She had somehow found out about it already and kept saying how sorry she was. I couldn't figure out how she knew because I didn't know my mother knew.

I just kept rationalizing and thinking, "Oh, well, somebody else will come along. I've always had all these guys." I couldn't stand to think of what really had happened. My mother took me to dinner, and we met one of her friends, who asked about Paul. I realized then that he was the best one I ever knew. There seemed to be no future at all without him. My mother tried to make me feel better and said something would work out, but I couldn't imagine it.

I asked her to take the ring and give it to Paul's friend, who was dating Rinda. I couldn't face giving it back myself. I went back to the apartment with Debbie, thinking my life had ended.

HER MOTHER'S STORY:
Handling the Breakup

I tried to figure out how to return to Paul the ring that had been so precious. I wanted to comfort him too. The whole nightmare swirled around me and careened me into non-action. I went home and wrote in my journal:

Wed., June 6, 1973, 1 A.M.—Oh, Mother, what I'd give to have you here! I need you to talk to maybe more than I ever have. Tonight Paul told Becky he didn't want to get married. She said to me, "I thought it was too good to be true, that someone would really want to marry me." Oh, Becky, poor, dear, stumbling, lost Becky—for a brief, so brief, shining moment, a feeling of being somebody—of being wanted, of planning, being "first." Tonight she gave me the ring that was her prize—to give back to Paul. And poor Paul—sad, groping, loving, trying to be the altruist, the savior—where are you wandering? Are you relieved? Broken? Uncertain? How will you manage? I can tell Becky in a dozen ways that it's better to know now, that there are other paths, that her life is just opening, that I love her, that she's worthwhile and full of promise, but it's all hollow-sounding as I realize I never could get started "working on the wedding" for all of my undisclosed and frantic misgivings. What now? Where, how? How? . . . . Today started out just fine, but always underwritten with unease. Intuition [has to be] the prime mover. What can I give her for sustenance?

Dark before the Light

I went back and talked to Debbie. She was very under-standing. Mostly, she just listened. Deep down, I felt that I could survive. I had come far enough along that I had a degree of self-esteem, so I knew I could figure out some-thing. Paul was the perfect person for me to marry. I loved him; I knew I loved him, but I had developed a way of escaping problems so that I would be okay and functional. With the help of lithium and imipramine, I was able to block out any deep feeling. Without this, I know I would have been suicidal.

To protect myself from the pain, I was trying to make it seem as though I didn't care. Debbie had to leave to do something, I don't even remember what. So when there was a knock on the door, I ignored it. The door opened. It was Paul. Smiling, he said, "Let's get married tonight. Let's elope."

I sat up, but I couldn't let myself believe what I was hearing. I probably said something like "You're kidding," very incredulously. I held back and wouldn't let him get close to me. I was still afraid to trust him. Then he started talking, and I asked him lots of questions, like Why did you change your mind? He said that he went home and talked to his father, and his father made him realize that it had been a mistake to break it off. Then he went for a ride with Adriane in his old Volkswagen and thought about his life and what he wanted to do. And he decided that he loved me and that marrying me was the right thing to do.

He hugged me tightly, and I was convinced. He said he would get the ring from his friend, and we would be engaged again.

Three days later, we were sitting in his car, and we started kissing, and he said he had it all worked out so we could get married on Saturday. He said he could not stand to be engaged any longer, that engagement was like no-man's-land. I realized that I felt the same way, it was like being in limbo.

That was Thursday night. We had only a little more than thirty-six hours to get everything ready. It felt like being in a whirlwind. I had no idea what it took to put a wedding together. I called my mom, and she said I should talk to Dr. Grosser. He said, "Fine." Then Paul and I went to talk to our parents. His were asleep, but we walked into their room and told them. They were really happy. Then I went alone to my house while Paul was taking care of details. My dad was already in bed, so I told my mother down in my old room where we had had so many talks. I must have looked ecstatic, because she shook her head and started to cry and hug me. Then she realized the wedding was going to be the next day and began planning.

PAUL'S STORY 1988:

I guess they were a short three years' worth of "courtship." And from the time I met Becky until we got married, I didn't think of her as sick in any serious or permanent way, but just confused and messed up. She lacked a solid foundation, you might say. I remember thinking on our first couple of dates that this girl is too fragile in her self-esteem and strung way too tight over a self-conception that can only snap.

After the interim between our second and third dates— about four months when we both left home for different destinations—I found my vague suspicions were correct. Our "third date" was at the psychiatric ward of LDS Hospital. Her looks were entirely different. She looked basic, fundamental, homemade, and ready or getting ready to try again at the question of who she was. In terms of where I was in life at the time, her being sort of melted-down bronze awaiting new casting was very fortuitous, because I was not unlike that myself. I'm a baby boomer. There were about twenty-six boys my age within a few blocks of where

154

I spent my first eighteen years on the planet [Salt Lake City]. I was rarely alone during my youth. Distraction was the norm. By age nineteen, I was ready for a big change, and Becky Thayne was it. We helped re-form each other.

Though I wouldn't have verbalized it at that time, I was beginning to discover that the real me, a mature me, was more intellectual than social and far more spiritual than intellectual. In simple terms, this means it is my nature to give priority to the promptings of my heart over the logic of my head. And to give total weight to my heart and head while giving no weight to being in step with society. It is within this frame of mind (or frame of being) that I met Becky, dated her, married her, and live with her and the kids to this day.

Therefore, though novel and interesting, there was nothing uneasy [about the fact], from my point of view, that our second date through maybe our fifteenth date took place at the psychiatric wards of the LDS and University of Utah hospitals. The fact is those were very exhilarating and exciting times for me, because it was so apparent that my heart was really onto something. Somehow I was honing in on the beam. That describes very well how I actually felt— on the warm and cozy beam of the heart that didn't require any effort for me to stay on. I had a sense of floating through life. In short, as would dawn on me at a conscious level a short time before our marriage, powers beyond me set this whole thing up. All I would do was go along with it. Becky Thayne was my destiny.

Wedding day at the cabin

CHAPTER 12

The Wedding

Miracle

I remember Paul's coming and getting me the next morning. We went and had blood tests done and then got the marriage license. It felt as if Paul was in total control, and I loved it. I had nothing to worry about as long as I was with him. All that mattered in the whole world was that I loved him and we would be married the next day.

He took care of everything. I didn't even know until the next day that he had ordered flowers and rented a tuxedo for the ceremony. Paul and I talked about whom to invite and who would marry us. Paul was raised in the Lutheran church, but he had no close ties to it. I had always liked our Mormon bishop, Spence Nilson, and he seemed like the logical person to ask to perform the ceremony. We both knew we wanted to be married at the cabin with very few people in attendance besides our closest families, maybe about thirty. I invited only two friends, Debbie and Kathy, and Paul felt too rushed to invite any friends. He just wanted to get married and start our new life.

Saturday morning, June 9, was a gorgeous day. At the cabin it was green all around outside, and there was light coming into the screened porch where the ceremony was to take place. I felt as if I was walking on air, that everything was right and that I would be taken care of. For the first time in years, eating and throwing up weren't foremost in my thoughts. Little did I know that this would be the end of my problem with that terrible illness that had controlled and ruined my life. I knew that Paul would love me even if I gained weight and that I didn't have to battle being too heavy anymore. I gave myself to him and felt that to throw up would be betraying the trust that we had after this day. Also, I knew that I couldn't get away with it, living with him and trying to hide my awful secret.

I remember putting on my white dotted swiss wedding dress that my mother and I had bought months before. She and I were alone in the bedroom with the high roof and rafters, where I used to giggle and tell stories with my sisters and resist going to sleep when I was a little girl. All I knew was that here on my wedding day I could not remember ever being so happy.

When I came out on the porch, Paul was waiting, and my sisters were playing their violins and flute. I know that all my relatives were around, but I felt suspended, as if there were only Spence and Paul and me in a little bubble. It seemed as though the world had gone away while Spence said some lofty and beautiful words of encouragement and inspiration. When Paul kissed me, it seemed almost like a fairy tale. He was extremely handsome in his tuxedo, like the "prince" I had imagined I would deserve when I was grown up.

After the ceremony, we had a lot of fun joking with the relatives and having everyone say congratulations. I had been sick for so long that it almost seemed like someone else they were talking to. I didn't feel right getting all that positive attention. I had been removed from everyone for so long that I really didn't feel like a person. It would be a long time before I would feel comfortable with myself, either alone or with people. Not only was this the beginning of Paul's and my life together, it was also the beginning of my becoming a person on my own. At this point, I was free to discover the world in a whole new way.

Some of the family gave us money, since they hadn't had time to buy a gift, and that was the beginning of our savings toward a house. Most of my friends' parents spent so much on their weddings that they didn't have any funds to offer afterward. We felt fortunate to have our parents give us money toward a down payment on a house instead of a large wedding. We would be the first of our friends to buy a home. But that was not what I was thinking about then. I remember throwing my bouquet as we were leaving. I tossed it over my shoulder and was gone so fast I don't even know who caught it.

We drove off in my little green Pinto to a Sweetwater condo on Bear Lake. The drive was carefree, happy, and lots of fun. We were ecstatic, on cloud nine. Our whole honeymoon was blissfully exhausting. There was a pool and a beach and a good restaurant, and I didn't have to worry about what I ate or did. It couldn't have been better.

HER MOTHER'S STORY:
The Wedding

When had I ever been so happy? Becky and Paul, Paul and Becky. And Becky beaming. That night of agony and ecstasy when Becky had said she would really decide in the morning, it was apparent that there was no question. I was so busy, it was four days before I could write about it in my journal.

Sunday, June 10, 4:30 P.M. At the cabin—Who'd believe it? Who could imagine that four days later Becky and Paul would be married and off on a honeymoon? Really, who'd believe? I lie here on this always dear, now beloved, porch looking at yesterday's geraniums that bedecked the wedding, and try to seep in the realization that it has all happened. Thurs. night Becky sent the ring back via Gary (I didn't want to be intermediary!) and she and I went to dinner. Something electrified Paul, and he hunted Becky up (after dinner with me and going "home" to stay with Debbie), told her he couldn't stand it any longer, and wanted to elope. She called me, Dr. Grosser, me—decided to decide in A.M. By Fri. 7 P.M., they were ready. Paul had seized the day, arranged everything. So we had a wedding—a splendid wedding—at 2 P.M. Sat. June 9th on this porch with [Bishop] Spence [Nilson] pronouncing, and Becky & Paul, in dotted swiss wedding dress and ruffled tuxedo, looking out onto green and stream with clear smiles and peaceful eyes.

I even had time to think about the miracle and put it in at least a little perspective.

Is happiness bred by spontaneity, impulse, extravagant audacity? If so, they will make the green world true. Oh, bless that they do. It will be a different world for them. As Paul quipped, "Scrambled Tab for breakfast." Scrambled maybe everything—and confused, according to imposed standards. But for them? Who can know but Paul, who kisses and holds her, just what's in it for him. Ah, so. Who can know? Who can even suppose what's in anything for anyone without that? . . .

And for the rest of us, how had it been? How would it be?

So now it's summer. Today is a quiet, lonely day. Having met yesterday's emergency, with all stunned but marshaled, Mel just fine in summoning his courage and his shovel to clear and clean, pleased eventually at their happiness, resilient on suggestion, tired but relieved. [I was up

*all night making open-faced sandwiches with friend Jan
Nilson, sisters-in-law, cousins making cookies.] The girls
all in a daze, but helping, of course, making their music on
violins and flute, finally relaxed and satisfied that it was
good for Becky & Paul & therefore everyone.*

*All the families supportive, moved. Markosians mellow
and glad, nice. Big switch from the day before when they
thought Paul had walked out and they were devastated.
Their love for Becky is sweet and reassuring. . . . "Mut"
everywhere. She would have smiled. Did we do all right,
Mother? Does Becky know how much it meant? Putting
on her dress in the bathroom, fixing her veil, watching her
look at Paul after he kissed her so gently, seeing a family
begin. Wistful, aching joy. Unbelievable release?*

Little wonder that the happiness grew into everything
else we did:

*Tues. June 12, 7 A.M. The Homestead. Birds. Birds. How
many out there? All declaring the day. Like last night,
hilarious reminiscing with thirty-one of us [at an extended
family party]. . . . Birds, sing for them as I swing into
rackets, saddles, grass. . . . Becky and Paul, how is your
time together? This first time really together?*

And they brought their "happily ever after" home with
them.

*Midnight Thurs. June 14 . . . Becky and Paul are glow-
ing—can't stop grinning. Paul in his PiKA [fraternity
tennis] shorts and smooth tan showed us proudly through
their ap't last night, full of his furniture and plants. Becky
just beams and loves him. Oh, let it last—be good!*

They continued. And their peace became a whole new state of being for all of us. I was born again.

Friday, June 29, noon . . . This summer has been so absolutely glorious! Becky and Paul seem so happy. Now they can't seem to be apart—even in the next room. What a switch! It fills me to watch them. . . . I have never felt so at peace, so like the tomboy who romped these trails in pure abandon. No summer in years has allowed me this freedom to mosey through the day doing exactly what whim and allegiance and being native draw me to.

Whatever else lay ahead, we could manage. Even though it would take another three months for Becky to be completely free of her throwing up, the thorough cure had begun.

CHAPTER 13

And They Lived Happily . . .

Nesting

We came home and got settled in the apartment that I had rented before to live in with Debbie. Paul got a job driving a delivery truck for Wycoff while he continued school. He worked weekends with me at the university switchboard, where I worked full-time. Contrary to the way many marriages are the first year, ours was idyllic. It was a surprise when we found out that I was pregnant three months after we were married. But we were really happy and excited. We had thought that we would wait to start a family, but we knew that we could get by and make things work. The happiness we found when our little boy was born in May 1974 started a whole new era in my life.

While I was pregnant, I didn't take lithium or imipramine, and I was happily surprised that I felt normal. I wasn't even nauseated. The birth of Nicholas Thayne Markosian brought me more happiness than we could ever have imagined.

Babies

The summer was not without relapses: *"Thurs. July 19, Paul wonders about Becky's sleeping so much. Depression? They still seem silly and happy—and he says so, says he loves it all. Oh, hope, hope."* But mostly, *"July 28th . . . Becky and Paul for dinner. Paul now the one telling Becky what and when—only her now doing it, deferring to his every suggestion."*

But the happiness was real, and long-lasting. From month to month, it was better and better. In September, they announced that they would have a baby in the middle of May. Wonderful! But pregnancy also meant no lithium or imipramine for all those months. Who could have imagined that instead of suffering dire effects, Becky would be more herself than she had been since she was ten. Whatever hormones and chemistries changed, Becky took on having a baby with vim and smiles. She and Paul bought an old house for almost nothing—thanks to her dad's real estate savvy—and they worked like professionals fixing it up. They both worked nights at the university switchboard, and Paul finished his degree in English.

In February, Rinda married Jim, and Becky stood as her matron of honor with her other sisters, beaming and baby-big. She was twenty-two and a half and back from a treacherous journey—whole, confident, and happier than I could ever remember her being.

The coming of Nicky that May was a stellar event. Was there ever a more wanted or darling baby? Paul played Beethoven for him as they lay on the living room floor, and Becky nursed the tiny baby with fond assurance. At two months, instead of feeling the more common postpartum depression, Becky began to get manic. She could work till 2 A.M. and still be awake to nurse the baby at three. Dr. Grosser told Becky that it was time to stop nursing and get back on lithium and imipramine, and that did the trick. Apparently, she would need the balancing the drugs gave her body for some time yet. Actually, Becky took both drugs until the spring of 1988; since then, she has needed only the lithium and has found it totally effective.

Her next pregnancy, with Richard, in 1975, was exactly like her first: no medication, perfect adjustment of hormones, no problems. (Dr. Grosser has suggested that perhaps not only is her chemistry different during pregnancy, but the chemistry of the baby might also cause some changes.) Becky took to mothering as she had to nursing and seemed to thrive on keeping a home. We teased her that since she could have babies like this, she should have a dozen.

Eventually, Becky needed more challenge and began engineering the fixing up of the house next door for sale. Through that and the propitious sale of their own home, she and Paul were able to parlay their profits into buying the home they have now lived in for twelve years. Michael was born seven years later and became for the other boys and Paul, as well as for Becky, the family playmate.

BECKY'S STORY:

Happiness and a Temporary Relapse

When we lived in our little white house on First Avenue, I stayed wonderfully happy. I had control over all areas of my life and loved having a home of our own with Nicky and Richard to play with and love. Right before Nicky was born, the people at the switchboard had a big quitting party for me. After leaving my job, I always found plenty to do at home, with creative projects or remodeling our house and the one next door that we bought for very little and expected to resell for a profit. I had no worries or cares and just loved being a young mother. Even though Nicky and Richard were only nineteen months apart, I still had my freedom if I needed it by getting baby-sitters or trading with friends or family.

Paul had writing jobs with a large advertising company, then with a grocery chain, and later with a TV station. He loved to play with his two boys and also helped with the remodeling we were doing. We spent a lot of time at home and didn't seem to need much else to make us happy.

Six years after we were married, we moved into the home we live in now, after making a huge profit on our First Avenue house. We sold it in 1979, when real estate was booming in Salt Lake. Paul still wanted to write, and for a time he quit his job and wrote stories, a novel, and some screenplays. He took a writing class and put a typewriter in our basement; often he went to his mother's house, where he could have quiet. This worried me a lot because we had little income at the time. His parents were worried, too, and they expressed this to him; but when we got too far into debt, they helped us out.

Then Paul himself realized that it was totally unrealistic to think he could make a living by doing freelance writing, and he got a job in real estate. He worked very successfully as a salesman for my dad for three years. Then he went on his own with another company until my dad had triple bypass heart surgery and decided to sell his building and his business. In 1987, Paul bought the company and took it over.

In 1985, when Paul listed a large apartment complex for his father, I got involved with fixing it up and having it painted so that they could sell it. I was also taking a class at the university on how to audition, because my children had been in TV commercials and the producers had asked me to audition for a mother role. I felt I needed more energy to manage all that I was working on, and I also felt distant from my usual interests at home. I had talked to Dr. Grosser about changing my medication. He gave me a different antidepressant to try, Desyrel, and within a week I felt totally different. I felt myself leaving reality again. In my drama class, we were supposed to enact parts of the Holocaust. I was to take the part of a Jewish woman about to be gassed. I was overwhelmed with emotion I had never felt or imagined before. I was learning what acting was really about—becoming another person and actually feeling what that person must have felt. It was too much for me to stand. For a week, I couldn't get over that new emotion, even after I left class, and I kept going back to it in my mind.

But I think the "point of no return" for me was when I had a crew digging to find a leak in a pipe at the apartment complex. One of the men cut the telephone cable to the hospital just up the hill and cut off their service. Suddenly, there were representatives from the phone company and the insurance company questioning me about why we hadn't checked on where we were digging. All I could do was apologize and feel helpless.

Also, I had borrowed my mother's car. She was in California with my sister, who was having a baby. The battery was dead, and I was stranded at the apartment. I remember walking to a small park down the street and just praying that I would be able to pull through this and be okay. I needed my mother more than I had in years, and she wasn't there to rescue me. But I was so involved with my problems that I didn't even consider calling her in California.

I knew that I needed help, but I couldn't talk to Paul. Maybe I was afraid to admit that this was happening. My mother was the one who knew me the best, and I thought she could help me get through this very difficult time. I must have been a lot better than in the years past because I recognized I was in trouble. When my mother got home—the next day—I went with her to see Dr. Grosser. In three weeks—with the help of Trilofon, an antipsychotic drug, and, of course, lithium—I was able to get back to taking care of the kids and the house. The final "cure" was a weekend trip to St. George in southern Utah that my mother and my mother-in-law sponsored for just Paul and me. It was like being on another honeymoon. I was tired a lot that summer but relieved that I had come out of it okay and hadn't had to go to the hospital at all.

Since then, I've been fine and have felt great as long as I do things within reason. In fact, I've never felt better. I have learned to monitor my own medication and have never even been tempted to binge or throw up. If I accidentally forget to take a lithium pill, I feel a rush of heaviness in my head that reminds me to take it. Sometimes I wish I didn't have to be dependent on a pill to function, but then I think, What if I had diabetes and needed insulin? I know I'm one of the lucky ones that lithium works for.

HER MOTHER'S STORY:

Happiness and a Temporary Relapse

Artistic yearnings sent Becky to learning how to do stained glass, and Paul to writing in every spare moment. Becky stayed stable through ups and downs of employment, and Paul grappled with the realities of making a living for five. To help with income, Becky took on a huge job of redoing an apartment complex with Paul's architect brother, at the same time that she was meeting crises in her extended family and going back to school. After fourteen years of the same medication, she asked Dr. Grosser to try something different. She felt that the lithium was fine but that the imipramine was leaving her "flat."

He agreed to a change in medication—to Desyrel. I didn't know anything about it. Just before that change, I spent eleven days in California with our fourth daughter, Dinny, awaiting her first baby. We tried to call Becky to tell her of the arrival of the new little girl, but we never could reach her. And she didn't call—all strong clues that things were not right.

The night I got home, I called Becky at midnight. She answered the phone and said, "Oh, Mom, I think I'm having a nervous breakdown." She probably was. I talked to Paul, who seemed to have noticed the changes but felt unsure of what to do. The next morning, Becky and I were in Dr. Grosser's office. He promised her that she would not have to go back into the hospital if she would agree to stay at our house and have us supervise her medication and behavior. Paul and the boys would have to manage without her for a while. Paul's mother took care of Michael, the easiest little boy ever, and she and I arranged for a woman to help with the others at home.

Fortunately, this took only three weeks. It was scary, but it was also heartening to know that, with the right medication, Becky could be just fine. The recurrence had been of the manic state. Becky's battle with bulimia and anorexia was apparently a thing of the past, never to trouble her again.

That manic incident took place seven years ago. Dr. Grosser says that the likelihood of another such episode becomes more and more remote as Becky puts greater distance between herself and the recurrence. She now takes only lithium, and she may have to do this for the rest of her life. Becky stays fit as well as trim, knows when she has to rest, and exercises her way out of tensions.

Dr. Grosser's assessment of the treatment of Becky, looking back from February 1990:

The long-term treatment of Becky dealt with three different conditions: the bipolar (manic-depressive) illness, the eating disorder, and the personality difficulties of which the shoplifting early on was the most serious manifestation [and about which she, at the time, demonstrated only apathy]. The bipolar illness, although to outward appearances the most serious, was the easiest to control, since lithium carbonate has been shown to be an excellent treatment for this condition.

It was decided to deal with the eating disorder and personality issues with a combination of family and behavior therapy, using as co-therapists myself and Dr. Steven Zlutnick, an accomplished psychologist with extensive experience in behavior therapy. Becky was diagnosed as both bulimic and anorexic, because, through her bingeing and purging, she tried to maintain an unrealistic weight, at one time asking me if she would look better at 94 pounds. When she took the laxatives, she would get dehydrated, so that when she ate or drank again, she would become bloated, would gain five or six pounds in a day, and then panic and call me. Dr. Zlutnick and I met with Becky and her family once a week from March to June 1972.

Since Becky, like many patients with manic depressive illness, suffered from intermittent bouts of depression (lithium carbonate acts as a better preventer of mania than of depression), in September, imipramine, an antidepressant, was added to her treatment regimen. The use of this medicine was extremely fortuitous. Not only did it alleviate her depression, but most probably it helped to reduce the intensity of the bulimic episodes. Subsequent studies by a number of researchers have shown that imipramine as well as other antidepressants significantly reduce the frequency of bingeing and purging episodes in bulimic patients.

Becky is now a vibrant, functional, extremely attractive woman, wife, and mother, plus a wage earner and taxpayer, who likely will need to continue indefinitely on medication of lithium carbonate, with blood levels drawn annually to ensure its efficacy. When under extreme stress, she is alert enough to her responses that she can monitor intermittent medication of Trilofon to alleviate agitation, a condition experienced only once since her recovery from a relapse five years ago. Tranquilizers like Valium could not accomplish the same end.

Improvement in her condition, then, could be attrib-

uted to a number of factors: appropriate medication, family and behavior therapy, continued support by her family, the stabilizing influence of Paul, her future husband, in her earliest and most acute episode, and the basic spiritual strength in Becky herself.

Bernard Grosser, M.D.
Professor and Head of Psychiatry
University of Utah School
of Medicine

Today

In September 1989, after taking classes to certify as a real estate agent, I passed the national and state tests and received my license. Taking the exam was traumatic for me. The only classes I had taken since college had been in art or stained glass, so actually dealing with facts and figures and detailed information was scary for me. Passing the exam meant that I had succeeded in conquering a fear that I had had for many years.

My life has changed considerably. I feel as if I have graduated from the relatively limited life of being at home, raising my children, being with my husband, playing, and doing my stained glass as I recovered myself. Those years of physical exercise and artistic productivity fed me so that I now feel ready to get outside myself and my domestic concentration.

I began working as personnel manager and co-owner at the real estate brokerage, Thayne and Associates, which Paul took over from my dad about three years ago. To be in charge of sixteen agents and recruiting new ones was challenging and somewhat overwhelming at times. It was a whole new world for me. I've loved the excitement of meeting new people and being in charge. But it is difficult to deal with the disappointments that are inherent in this business—failing sales, problems with different temperaments and ethics. Now I am selling too. I still have a lot to learn and am taking classes and seminars to improve my skills.

My day starts with excitement at 6:30 A.M., as I get the boys off to school. Now Michael is in third grade and is gone all day, so this is the perfect time for me to be starting my career. I go to the office at about 9 and greet our secretary. I do detail work until I get busy on the phone arranging appointments or working with the salespeople. I know I'm making a difference in the office, and Paul likes my being there and is usually very encouraging.

Of course, there has to be some adjustment to my being so busy away from home, but the boys are glad I'm working and actually help at home a lot more than they used to.

Now that I'm in the world of business, I find I have to watch how I deal with difficult situations. Somehow, the stress of my job is much greater than any stress I have had since my recovery. In the past, Paul and I restored some houses to sell for profit, but I dealt with those challenges a lot more confidently because I knew that I could handle the problem. Now I am in a field where there are so many things I don't know that I feel pressured to learn all the time. Often I have to take time off to swim or just go home and take a nap or do some stained glass. But I know now what it takes to relax and get back to myself. I like my work and I like me. It feels wonderful.

HER MOTHER'S STORY:

Becky Today

Since that three-and-a-half-year struggle that ended more than eighteen years ago with the marriage of Becky and

Richard, Paul, Nick, Becky, and Michael Markosian

Paul and Becky's start on a new life, she has become a woman *I* look to now. I see her functioning in a healthy household with Paul and her secure and easygoing boys. They seem to like other people and themselves, and they get along wherever they go.

Becky is becoming very much her own woman, even with Paul. As she becomes a more and more successful saleswoman, he recognizes that she has talents in dealing with people, and he apparently is willing to turn over to her some of the responsibilities in the office.

But way beyond any of this obvious making of the good life, Becky seems to be finding a life inside herself that she can draw on in either quiet or turbulent times. She is a thoroughly loving person, and it shows. No one is a nonperson to her. She keeps herself beautiful through reasonable eating, exercise, and care of her hair and complexion. But more than external beauty shines out of her face and eyes: Becky has a beguiling gentleness about her.

Because she is sure of herself, she now can enjoy the mature comfort of caring about others. She takes on the tending of Paul's sister Adriane, fixes meals for a sick neighbor, makes a stained glass window for a friend with a new house, tends her sisters' or neighbors' children, has a job in her church, and most recently, has undertaken the writing of this book in the hope of helping someone else. Honesty is a given in anything she is involved with, and no one I know is more trusted.

For her sisters, Becky is there with compassionate understanding or homemade ice cream and overnight tending of a niece or nephew or two. For her dad, she is now a fellow realtor, and he is someone she looks to as a senior consultant and often a companion at a movie or in the swimming pool. To him, she is "very bright and has a way with people that is rare." Her friends are many and varied and in steady touch. For me, she is my fun, my sweet companion in everyday doings, who pampers me and rescues me in any crisis.

More, she is the courageous girl-become-woman who has overcome and now wants to help anyone else who needs to do the same. I respect as well as love her with all my heart.

Becky, second from the left,
and the Thayne family
(Paul is standing behind her).

Conclusion:
We Learned

When Paul and I get away together, we realize how good we are for each other, and we feel that we have stability in our marriage and a good feeling about the future.

I like and respect his family and appreciate how good they have been to me. They are very giving, considerate people, and they make me feel as if I'm good for them too.

With my Thayne family, I feel totally comfortable also. I have an excellent relationship with all of my sisters. I feel that we will always be close, although three of them live far away. Since my marriage and my recovery, we're on good terms and share our feelings like best friends. I love them all dearly.

My illnesses are far removed from my life now, and I honestly feel like a new and different person. My father is a great inspiration and support at the office. He is very well respected in the real estate industry and has an excellent reputation. With him too, the past is over and gone, and our relationship is a good one. He always goes out of his way to help me and build up my confidence. His shared knowledge of real estate is amazing to me, and I think we'll have a lot of good years together. He's a darling grandpa and regularly takes the boys to basketball games, boating, swimming, or the movies.

To me, my mother is "Wonder Woman." She still astounds me when I hear her speak and inspire a huge group of people, or when I read her writing, especially her poetry. She has a very real gift that allows her always to see the best in people and situations and lets her deal with things with compassion. We all—my kids, too— would just as soon be with her as with anyone in the world.

I cringe when I think of what misery I caused her during those awful, painful years (for both of us). She could have disowned me or sent me somewhere, and I would never have recovered.

Growing up with my mother wasn't easy for me because I wasn't driven or energetic or talented, as she was. It was hard too because some of my friends, especially one, also looked to her as a mother. Sometimes it was difficult even to begin to live up to being her oldest daughter, but I certainly have come to appreciate her now.

She is my best friend. She believed in me through everything, and I feel that without her constant encouragement I would never have made it. She is my hero— and I mean that. She is an incredible woman, and I love her with all my heart.

HER MOTHER'S STORY:

In May 1986, Mel had heart surgery, a triple bypass. He did well, but it was close. The morning of his surgery, I scribbled off a poem that Becky had asked me to write for a mothers-and-daughters party she was partly in charge of. The title, "Kaleidoscope," seemed to epitomize where we were and how we had gotten there.

Kaleidoscope

You spin the glass, the colors fall
continuous as seasons—
diamonds, squares, circles, walls
spread and change like reasons

why perpetual the ups, the downs,
the interchange of spectrum.
You want to hold the patterns shown
yet how can you expect them,

myriad as sands in motion
touched at will to hold?
And who would want the sky or ocean
fixed in any mold?

What hand can shift my gloom to grace
between sun up and down?
What trials soon will interface
with blessings, smiles with frowns?

This too shall pass, these colors, shapes,
this day's configurations;
the secret is to spin and wait
till loss is restoration.

Things happen, and things change. Probably the most significant lesson for me has been to take one day at a time, to know that changes will come—good ones and not so good ones. But the real secret is to take time to look back at the big picture. Now I can see that both Becky and I, through those years and these pages, have been "born again, free" of those diseases. It is a wondrous thing—a still fragile thing in many ways but also a sturdy one.

Perhaps the arrival that I sense can be compared to looking at the big stained glass window that Becky made for our entry hall in 1983, thirteen years after her coming home so ill from Seattle.

By 1983, Becky had been married for eleven years, had three young sons, and had become astonishingly able with stained glass. Her work was commissioned by restaurants, stores, and home owners, as well as being exhibited in galleries. Stained glass had become her profession.

Becky did our stained glass from a photo she took of a scene she knew we loved—a great pine tree overlooking the Salt Lake Valley and the far Oquirrh Mountains, with sky and a few clouds above them. Everything about the window changes with light.

When our lights are on inside, the deep, rich colors of that sunset scene show clear to the street. From inside, the window changes every hour with the light. In the morning, it sends prisms dancing on walls and staircase. On a cloudy day, the glass glows with color. Even at night, the streetlight and sometimes the moon mute the colors.

I never look at this window without thinking of Becky, and I think, with love and gratitude, of a need to keep a large perspective. I realized this very clearly about Becky in one blessed moment three years ago.

A freakish accident on the freeway left me with eight fractures in my forehead, cheek, temple, and jaw, and with my upper teeth damaged. Rushed to the emergency room of the hospital, I never lost consciousness, nor did I cry or even feel pain. I had had a death experience. Except for Jim, my plastic surgeon son-in-law, who was driving the car through which a crowbar crashed on the freeway, all of my family was uncharacteristically out of town. I was lying all alone between procedures, waiting to be temporarily stitched up and then iced to wait for surgery, when Becky appeared in the door of the semidark x-ray room, silhouetted against the light. She came to where I lay on the table, equipment and its findings hanging over me. With glass fragments still in my eye, which was almost sealed with swelling, in that distant dark I felt her take my hand. She was like the window—a presence, a reassurance, with the fragility of glass, connections of lead, backed by the strength of structural support to last forever. She was the brown earth, the green tree, the blue sky, the gray and white clouds. She was life.

The configurations of light will change. Always. But Becky's view and mine will be broader and kinder, full of understanding for having found healing—and hope.

Afterword

Writing this book has been hard. We had put so much distance between us and those desperate years. To look back into letters and journals and search our memories made our story immediate, maybe even dramatic. Nothing could have meant more growth individually nor more connectedness. Our writing has been both catharsis and enlightenment, as our memories have been like wizened apples dropped in a strange elixir that plumps them up and offers them back whole and far too full of their original flavor.

But the price for realism has been high. The years of Becky's illness were years to be understood, accepted, forgiven—and put behind us. We both need to move on. Neither of us wants to become consumed with giving lectures, seminars, or private advice. If even one reader believes that the hope is there—as well as the disease—then we have succeeded. From now on, the book will have to be our voice. The following letter to Becky, dated February 24, 1990, illustrates how Becky's influence must move from personal contact to depending on the book for whatever help either of us might provide:

> *Five years ago one of my daughters had a manic-depressive (bipolar) episode similar to Becky's. Although knowing Becky in the neighborhood for a number of years, I had no knowledge of her past traumatic experiences. I only knew my wife and I were at the lowest point of our lives as we watched the sudden deterioration of our beautiful, sweet and talented 17-year-old, who at one moment had the world as her oyster and the next was in a mental ward of a local hospital. . . .*
>
> *Upon her release and the beginnings of her up-and-down recovery . . . a literal ray of hope came to my daughter by the name of Becky Markosian. As Becky at that time*

was considering telling her story in the form of a book, with the purpose to bring her hard-earned enlightenment to others, she took our daughter under her wing and, knowing better than anyone else what to do and say, did it—and we will be forever grateful. She taught her it was a physical ailment no different than an appendix attack or a bad cold and that it was not anything she or her parents had or had not done, but that it was an upset in the chemical balance in the brain, which left the victim unable to function normally until medications (thank God for recent discoveries) could gradually do their work. Becky taught her to play tennis and jogged with her and rebuilt her self-esteem, and the theme that kept coming through to our daughter and us was—if such a gorgeous, "has it all together" person like Becky went through this and is who she is today, everything will be all right. And I remember sighing with my first awareness of some relief after months of misery, and experiencing way deep inside, and for the first time since the ordeal began—HOPE. Sincerely, Gerald Peterson.

Then, after reading the manuscript:

This book should be in every hospital and library and in the hands of every parent and patient who is unwillingly introduced to bipolar, bulimia, anorexia, and other mental illnesses, when the victims and loved ones are suddenly dropped through their personal trapdoor to hell. It will help them face the facts and begin to deal with the problems and, gratefully, show them that others have been there and are back.

We have been astonished at how common Becky's problems—chemically caused instability and bulimia/anorexia—are, just among those people we know. Neither of us has ever mentioned this book without having someone tell about a loved one who has suffered or is now suffering in much the same ways that Becky did.

And always, the response to their hearing about Becky's story has been "I can hardly wait to read your book. Do you have some answers?"

The most significant answers we have found lie in getting help, competent help—soon. Becky's happy ending could never have come about without the aid of experts. If you would like to talk about the problems addressed in Becky's story, if you need help of any kind, if you would like a speaker to come to your group, *do not call us*. Instead, please call or write to one of the following, who know much more than we ever could:

Eating Disorders,
Anorexia Nervosa*
P. O. Box 102
Eugene, OR 97405
503-344-1144

NARSAD
(National Alliance for
Research on Depression
and Schizophrenia)
208 South LaSalle Street, Suite 1428
Chicago, IL 60604-1003
312-641-1666

National Depressive and
Manic Depressive Association
Merchandise Mart
Box 3395
Chicago, IL 60654
312-939-2442

NAMI
(Manic Depressive
National Alliance for
Mentally Ill)*
1901 No. Ft. Myer Drive, Suite 5000
Arlington, VA 22209-1604
703-524-7600

National Anorexia Aid Society*
P. O. Box 29461
Columbus, OH 43229
614-436-1112

National Association of
Anorexia and Associated
Disorders
Box 271
Highland Park, IL 60035
708-831-3438

*Local chapters listed in local phone books.

Besides this help, we are convinced that there is a power waiting to be tapped that will give you hope and may provide the final triumph over whatever mental illness or deadly disorder plagues you today. Private and personal, it is in that inner region where light and hope finally reside. We will be eternally grateful if the help you find allows you to be blessed—as we have been—with moving on.

In loving camaraderie,

Becky and her mother

FOR FURTHER READING

Erlanger, Ellen. *Eating Disorders: A Question & Answer Book about Anorexia Nervosa & Bulimia Nervosa.* Minneapolis: Lerner, 1988.

Gilbert, Sara. *Get Help.* New York: William Morrow, 1989.

Kolodny, Nancy J. *When Food's a Foe: How to Confront and Conquer Eating Disorders.* Boston: Little, Brown, 1987.

Landau, Elaine. *Why Are They Starving Themselves? Understanding Anorexia Nervosa and Bulimia.* New York: Julian Messner, 1983.

Lee, Essie and Richard Wortman. *Down Is Not Out: Teenagers and Depression.* New York: Julian Messner, 1986.

Levenkron, Steven. *Treating and Overcoming Anorexia Nervosa.* New York: Warner Books, 1982.

Maloney, Michael and Rachel Krantz. *Straight Talk about Eating Disorders.* New York: Facts on File, 1991.

Silverstein, Herma. *Teenage Depression.* New York: Franklin Watts, 1990.

ABOUT THE AUTHORS

Becky Thayne Markosian lives in Salt Lake City, Utah, with her husband and three young sons. This book is her story.

Twenty-one years ago, at nineteen, she had a three-year battle with manic depression, anorexia nervosa, and bulimia.

A first-time author, Becky Markosian wanted to write this book to help others who suffer from the same pain she knew and moved past.

For eighteen years she has been well, living a rewarding life as an artist of stained glass and recently as a successful real estate agent.

Emma Lou Warner Thayne, her mother, is a much published writer living in Salt Lake City with her husband of forty-two years. They are the parents of five daughters, five sons-in-law, and seventeen grandchildren. She is listed in *Contemporary Authors* and *A Directory of American Poets.*

Becky's illness was overwhelming, her recovery a chance to breathe again. Writing this book with her daughter has been one of the most challenging and fulfilling adventures of her life.